SWIMMING POOL BASICS FOR SERVICING PROFESSIONALS

LEARN THE BASICS, PASS THE EXAM &
START YOUR OWN SWIMMING POOL CLEANING BUSINESS

CONTENTS

INTRODUCTION

I want to thank you and congratulate you for downloading this book. This book is a must for all who are looking to start a pool servicing business and a great reference with new insights on all who are already in pool servicing business. It covers the basic foundation for someone getting into swimming pool servicing business.

There are thousands of swimming pools that need servicing every day. Many states mandate that the commercial pools are ONLY serviced by certified/licensed pool technicians.

It is important to note that the California Business and Practices Law, Section 704, requires a State Contractor's License for any job which totals $500 dollars or more in labor and materials. If you are looking to make massive amount of money servicing commercial pool you must start here! Did you know that most jurisdictions require that you have your Certified Pool Technician license before you can service any commercial swimming pool? To become certified, you must pass a one-time examination. To maintain the certification, technician must pay a yearly renewal fee thereafter.

This book will teach you on how to pass and obtain your pool technician license. This e-book contains all of the topics covered on the exam and lays foundation of servicing commercial swimming pool. It can also help in your private certification courses such as National Swimming Pool Foundation or Association of Pool & Spa Professionals. Both public and private pools in some jurisdiction must be serviced by a certified Swimming Pool Service Technician or Apprentice Technician license.

If you own a swimming pool business or manage a swimming pool business, this book can help you as well! It offers insights into what most regulatory agencies are look for during their inspections. It gives ideas on how you can recommend these services to your clients and grow your business. For swimming pool business owners this means specific ideas to grow your business.

If you are hiring new employees this book is a good guide recruitment guide to help your new employees get started.

If you are looking to start your own pool servicing business this book provides useful information and a great reference.

This book offers insight into basics of pool chemistry (pH, disinfectant, TDS, alkalinity, and other chemicals that are used in pool industry), recirculation system and other equipment that are commonly found in commercial pools. It outlines in detail the requirements by local enforcement agencies. This book covers basic pool calculations, formulas and practice test.

Public pools should have their chemical levels checked daily and should be serviced one to three times a week depending on the bather load. Heavily used public pools, such as at a health clubs, should have their chemical levels checked every hour and be serviced daily and they all need qualified technician to do this.

Maintenance is required on many levels including oils removal from tiles, repairing broken or illegible depth marker tiles, fixing loose ladder/stair handrails/grab rails, fixing broken or missing skimmer lids or deck valve lids, replacing missing or broken main drain covers, Ensuring a body hook with proper length pole, and a life ring with a proper length rope and approved proper signage at pools, etc.. I will provide detail requirement of above items and much more in the book. This will help your technician do more thorough inspection of the pool area and create even more business.

This book is also great book to have on your shelves if you have purchased or plan to purchase a house that has a pool and want to learn more about swimming pool in general.

Here is detail of what this book covers:

It will cover pool chemistry, filtration, maintenance, testing, and government regulations, pool calculation and many more:

- Disinfection, pH and stabilizer levels
- Clarity, bacteriological and chemical quality of pool water.
- General requirements for maintaining pools clean, sanitary and in good repair.
- Skimmers and their proper operation and maintenance.
- Required turnover rates.
- Flowmeters.
- Chlorine gas
- Breakpoint chlorination.
- Chlorine and bromine based products used to disinfect pool water.
- Methods of action of disinfectants in clarifying and sanitizing pool water.
- Advantages and disadvantages of various disinfectants, their properties and effects on pool water.

- Chlorine demand: Combined, total, and free available chlorine.
- Alternate methods of disinfection and treatment of pool water.
- Balance of pool water: Total alkalinity, calcium hardness and pH, and proper levels in pool water.
- Other chemicals used in pool maintenance including stabilizers
- Effects of corrosive and alkaline water
- Detrimental effects on health of improperly disinfected and balanced pool water
- Tests and proper use of test kits for measuring disinfectant residuals, pH and other chemical levels in pool water.
- Pool chemical safety
- Pool filters types, capabilities, sizing, cleaning and maintenance.
- Pool pumps, basic design, operation, characteristics, and maintenance
- Calculations: Volume of pool and spa
- Elevate or lower pH, alkalinity, and calcium
- Minimum flow rates, turnover rates, and filter sizes for public pools
- Saturation index

This book is a great resource and is filled with must know information if you are starting out in servicing pool. This is a very lucrative business with specialized niche, for all who take time to learn the basics, which this book will provide.

The information herein is offered for informational purposes solely, and is universal as so. The presentation of the information is without contract or any type of guarantee assurance.

The trademarks that are used are without any consent, and the publication of the trademark is without permission or backing by the trademark owner. All trademarks and brands within this book are for clarifying purposes only and are the owned by the owners themselves, not affiliated with this document.

CHAPTER 1:
IMPORTANCE OF DISINFECTION

Disinfection is the process of destroying living microorganisms and bacteria in sufficient numbers (by definition - 99.9%) to prevent the transmission of disease.

One of the most important part of a pool technician's job is to ensure safety of swimmers. One of the most vital is to ensure there is adequate disinfection to prevent disease and to provide safe pool water. Swimmers may bring many different contaminants into the pool from urine, blood, feces, bacteria, viruses, various chemicals from their skin and clothing, etc...

There are many health concerns that arise from swimming pool that are not properly maintained. Common parasites found from pool water that is not properly disinfected are Giardia and Cryptosporidium. These parasites along with others, along with poor pool conditions may lead swimmers to complain about burning of eyes, itching/pain in ear, nose, throat and skin that maybe result of an infection or pool conditions. More serious diseases can also manifest such as Hepatitis A, Norwalk Virus, Shigellosis, Cryptosporidiosis, Dysentery, Streptococcal, Sore Throat/Sinusitis, Legionnaires Disease, Typhoid Fever, Conjunctivitis, Ear /Urinary Tract Infections, Staph Infections, Granuloma, Impetigo / Dermatitis, Folliculitis, etc.

Ill maintained swimming pool can be easily spotted. A pool that has leaves, moldy tiles, cloudy water and algae growth. *(Algae is usually green, can also be black or yellow; plant like growth clinging onto floors and/or walls which can create* *slippery surfaces.).*There can be many cause for this such as improper chemical levels, damaged equipment, out of control bather load, inadequate filtration, etc.

Needless to say it is very important to have swimming pool that is well maintained. Disinfection and proper pool maintenance destroys many of these contaminants and helps keep the pool safe for swimmers.

A very obvious sign of lack of disinfectant is the growth of Algae. Algae growth in pools may indicate that chlorine residuals are not being continuously maintained. Algae growth is also stimulated by other conditions such as hot weather, sunlight, heavy bather loads, high TDS, rough finishes, low pH and scale formation. Besides being aesthetically undesirable, algae create a slipping hazard and can cloud the water. A major part of eliminating algae growth in pools can be accomplished by brushing the walls and floor with a nylon or stainless steel brush, and maintaining proper disinfectant levels. You can also look to purchasing Algaecide (copper or silver based), do a point contact treatment or super-chlorinate your pool. There are many Algaecides, chemicals that kill algae. Copper compounds are excellent algaecides but should be chelated to prevent staining of the pool walls and floor. Quaternary ammonium compounds are also used as algaecides but can cause foaming.

However your first defense should be to maintain proper chlorine levels.

CHAPTER 2:
CHLORINE

The most widely used disinfectant is Chlorine.

Chlorination is the most commonly used method of disinfection in residential and commercial swimming pools. Common forms of chlorine available in swimming pool ranges from liquid chlorine (sodium hypochlorite), Trichlor, Dichlor, Lithium hypochlorite and gas chlorite. Pure chlorine is a gas at room temperature and standard pressure.

Chlorine is two times heavier than air and is also toxic and corrosive. It is a strong irritant, so proper safety must be taken. Chlorine products should never be mixed with one another. It is important to closely follow the manufacturer's label on each chemical. Misuse of chemicals can injure the operator and swimmers. Mixing together some pool chemicals can cause dangerous gases to form, explosion, or fire. Mixing Trichlor with Calcium Hypochlorite or Lithium Hypochlorite will likely cause a violent explosion. As a rule, it is safer to add chemicals to water than to add water to chemicals.

In addition to disinfection, chlorine is a powerful oxidizer. Oxidation is the process of cleansing or purging the pool or spa of organic and nitrogen contaminants such as swimmer wastes, algae, and environmental pollutants. In simple terms, oxidation is the burning out process to convert complex organic or nitrogen compounds into simpler components that can eventually escape as an innocuous, insoluble gas such as carbon dioxide (Co_2), elemental nitrogen (N_2).

CHEMICAL REACTION OF CHLORINE IN THE POOL

When chlorine is first added to pool water it separates to form free chlorine. Soon, the free chlorine combines with impurities in the water such as ammonia to forms chloramines. Chloramines are considered to be combined chlorine. Combined chlorine is a weak disinfectant, has a strong chlorine odor and irritates the eyes. The ideal situation is to have zero combined chlorine in the pool. If the combined chlorine level gets higher than 0.2 parts per million (ppm); the pool is in need of super chlorinating (shocking). This is usually accomplished by increasing the chlorine residual to 5 - 10 parts per million or by adding 10x the amount of chlorine usually added. This results in destroying the combine chlorine to inert elements and leaving essentially free chlorine in the pool. This is called breakpoint (Adding enough free available chlorine to remove combined available chlorine and other waste compounds). After reaching breakpoint, any further addition of chlorine will result in a direct rise in free available chlorine. The actual amount of chlorine needed to remove all impurities from water is referred to as chlorine demand. Pools that have been super chlorinated should be allowed to return back to normal chlorine levels or at least 5ppm.

Free available chlorine (FAC) is chlorine that is free and available for disinfecting / oxidizing. It is most effective at killing microorganisms at low pH (7.0 - 7.2).

Combined Chlorine (CAC) is combined with a waste compound (compound with ammonia, nitrogen or other organic material). It is not a good disinfectant/oxidizer. It is also known as chloramine or trichloride and does have chlorine odor and can irritate eyes and skin. However most combined chlorine in a pool is Monochloramine. NH3 + HOCI > NH2CI + H2O. Combined chlorine forms more rapidly during heavy bather loads. You can add free available chlorine to remove combined available chlorine and other waste compounds.

To calculate the combined chlorine, subtract the free chlorine reading from the total chlorine reading.

Total Available Chlorine (TAC) is simply Free Available Chlorine (FAC) + Combined Available Chlorine (CAC).

FAC + CAC = TAC

FAC = 1.0 PPM

CAC = 0.5 PPM

TAC =1.5 PPM

Example; If a pool had 1.5 ppm of total chlorine and 1.0 ppm free chlorine, the amount of combined chlorine would be .5 ppm.

Ex) let's say the amount of free chlorine to add is 10 x combined chlorine level.

So if CAC = 0.7 ppm; Amount of free chlorine to add would be 10 x 0.7 ppm = 7 ppm.

Likewise If a pool had 3.0 ppm of total chlorine and 2.0 ppm free chlorine, the amount of combined chlorine would be 1.0 ppm.

When chlorine is added to pool water, it forms hypochlorous acid and hydrochloric acid.

The chemical equation for this reaction is: $Cl_2 + H_2O \rightarrow HOCl + HCl$. Hypochlorous acid or HOCL is the active disinfectant. Hypochlorite Anions are a weak disinfectant.

Hydrochloric acid is actually a by-product of the reaction that has no disinfectant properties. Hypochlorous acid is measured as free-chlorine residual.

HOCI (active disinfectant) can actually dissociate in water to become hydrogen ions (H+) and hypochlorite ions (OCI-), depending on the pH of the water. The lower the pH more HOCI, the higher the pH more OCI-.

The chemical equation for this reaction is: $HOCl \leftarrow \rightarrow H+ + OCl-$.

Thus pH has an effect on how strong disinfection is. The more acidic (lower) the pH, more hypochlorous acid remains in the water and more disinfection takes place. The more alkaline the pH, the more hydrogen Ions and hypochlorite anions form resulting in less disinfection. However it is important to know the ideal range of chlorine level, extreme on either end is not good.

In addition to the above reaction, Chlorine also combines with nitrogen compounds such as ammonia in pool water, to form chloramines or combined chlorine. Ammonia combines with hypochlorous acid to form monochloramine and water.

The chemical equation for this reaction is: $NH_3 + HOCl \rightarrow NH_2Cl + H_2O$.

CHAPTER 3:
CHARACTERISTICS OF WIDELY USED DISINFECTANTS

TRICHLORISOCYANURATES & DICHLORISOCYANURATES

(Trichlor and Dichlor) are organic chlorine compounds. In these compounds, chlorine molecules are attached to molecules of cyanuric acid (stabilizer). Trichlor has 90% available chlorine and a pH of 2.0 - 3.0. Dichlor has 60 - 65% available chlorine and a pH of 6.8. Therefore regular use of Trichlor or Dichlor requires the addition of an alkaline, such as soda ash, to raise the pH.

LIQUID CHLORINE

Sodium hypochlorite's convenient liquid form has made it a popular and economical chlorinating agent for residential and commercial pools. However the drawback is its instability. Sodium hypochlorite (liquid chlorine) has approximately 10 - 15% available chlorine and a pH of 13.0 or greater. It tends to raise pH, and regular use of liquid chlorine usually requires the addition of an acid to lower the pH. Approximately 8 ounces of acid will neutralize one gallon of liquid chlorine. Advantages of using liquid chlorine are low cost, easily stored, minimal danger to the operator, and ease of mixing with pool water. Liquid chlorine can be used to super-chlorinate / shock the pool, by mixing 1 gallon of liquid chlorine to 1 lb. of salt to pool water. It decomposes due to sunlight and heat, or over given time and does have the shortest shelf-life of all chlorine products.

The short shelf-life and increased levels of sodium (salt) in pool water makes it possible for scale formation if the pH is not controlled. As one can clearly see, increasing the storage temperature of sodium hypochlorite significantly increases its rate of auto decomposition. It requires cool, dark area for its storage to ensure peak performance. Sodium hypochlorite solutions ranging from 10 to 15ppm available chlorine by volume are available in one- gallon containers or larger volume carboys. Care must be exercised when handling large volumes of sodium hypochlorite; their bulkiness makes them difficult to handle. Residential pool owners and service agents using sodium hypochlorite have found direct pool application quick and convenient, while large, commercial pools requiring significant volumes and are usually equipped with a chemical metering pump that automatically delivers the slightly yellow liquid solution to the pool or spa recirculation system. It is a relatively simple set-up; and, yes, as with gas chlorine systems, sodium hypochlorite delivery can be automated with an ORP (Oxidation-Reduction Potention) chemical controller. No matter what application method, the chemistry is the same. Sodium hypochlorite reacts with water to produce HOCl and sodium hydroxide (NaOH); the latter being a very strong, basic (alkaline) molecule responsible for sodium hypochlorite's high pH. Consequently, acid must be added to reduce the pH. For larger pools, muriatic (or hydrochloric) acid is economical and effective. Residential pool owners frequently prefer sodium bisulfate; a dry, crystalline like acid with hygroscopic (water-absorbing) properties. Approximately one gallon of 20 muriatic acid is required to neutralize 4 to 5 gallons of averaged strength sodium hypochlorite. Because of smaller, less frequent applications, residential pool owners are advised to adopt pH and acid demand tests to determine the quantity of acid required. REMEMBER: For lowering pH, the acid should be diluted or dissolved prior to addition. Always add acid to plenty of cool water, and always use a clean (preferably white or clear) plastic container.

CHLORINE GAS

Chlorine gas (CI_2) is 100 active strength and 100 Available Chlorine Content (ACC), making it the highest available chlorine content of any product. Active strength refers to the actual percentage by weight of the sanitizer, while available chlorine content refers to the relative sanitizing and oxidizing strength. Chlorine gas (with ·its 100 ACC) is the reference compound for which other halogenated compounds are evaluated. Chlorine Gas has 100% available chlorine and an extremely low pH. Therefore it is necessary to continually add an alkaline, such as soda ash or caustic soda, into the pool to maintain the pH. Chlorine gas lowers pH of pool water, it is the most economical sanitizer, however it is can create toxic gas which makes it very dangerous and often its leak are hard to detect. It is a light green gas which is 2½ times heavier than air. Small leaks of chlorine gas can be detected using a 26 Baume (density scale) solution of ammonia that produces white smoke. Large leaks should only be repaired using an approved self-contained breathing apparatus. Advantages of using gas chlorine are low cost, indefinite shelf-life and effective disinfection and oxidizing properties. The major disadvantage is the dangers associated with use of the product. Very few public pools use gas chlorine for disinfection. Chlorine gas is usually present in pools with large volumes of water; it is pumped into the recirculation system at a controlled rate using a positive displacement type pump. Compressed gas chlorine cannot be used on public pools unless it is permanently installed on site, contained in a separate room, and dispensed through an approved chlorinator. "Gas shooting" from a portable unit is not allowed at public pools. Chlorine gas should also NEVER be used on residential pools.

Some of the properties includes are:

1. Toxicity and difficult to contain in the event of a leak.

2. Lack or experienced chlorine gas operators.

3. Additional insurance premiums incurred with its use.

4. Deterioration of equipment and property in and around equipment area.

Keep in mind that Chlorine gas reacts with water to produce free available chlorine (HOCl) and hydrochloric acid. For every pound of chlorine gas consumed, approximately one-half pound of hydrochloric acid is generated. Because of this, chlorine gas lowers the pH requiring the continuous and automated addition of sodium carbonate (soda ash) or sodium hydroxide (caustic soda). Pound for pound, chlorine gas is the most economical swimming pool sanitizer. Although economically attractive, the hazardous handling properties of this toxic gas has resulted in some foreign countries discontinuing its use in residential pool.

DRY CHLORINE

Calcium hypochlorite is a dry chlorine product with 65% available chlorine and raises pH of pool water. It usually comes in dry compound (granules and pellets), by adding calcium to water it increases its hardness. Due to increases in calcium hardness the product must be pre-mixed before adding it to pool water to prevent separation. It can also be used to super chlorinate pool. The advantage in using this product is its stability. Calcium hypochlorite was the primary method of residential and, to some extent, commercial pool disinfection prior to the introduction of stabilized chlorine, specifically trichloroisocyanuric acid. Calcium hypochlorite is available in granular or pellet form. The active strength and available chlorine content (ACC) of calcium hypochlorite are always the same. This equivalency can be verified by substituting in values in the previously mentioned available chlorine content (ACC) equation. Calcium hypochlorite is usually 65 active strength and available chlorine content. Although less soluble than lithium hypochlorite, calcium hypochlorite solubility of 21.7 grams per 100 grams of solution makes it ideal for shocking or continuous feeding applications. Its pH ranges between 11 and 12.Continuous use of calcium hypochlorite will increase calcium levels. This influence on calcium levels is due to calcium present in calcium hypochlorite. From a weight percentage perspective, calcium represents approximately 18.2 by weight of calcium hypo-chlorite (65). In simple and more understandable terms: The addition of two (2) pounds of 65 calcium hypochlorite to an 18,000 gallon pool introduces approximately 165 grams (0.364 lbs.) of calcium. In 18,000 gallons of water, this represents a 2.4 ppm increase in the calcium level.

This unavoidable addition of calcium can be constructively beneficial in geographical areas with soft water, but in hard water areas, the rapid buildup of calcium levels can cause rough scale deposits and filter calcification. Pool owners, operators, and service agents who use large amounts of calcium hypochlorite should check water hardness levels frequently. Calcium hypochlorite's strong oxidizer properties requires that it be handled with extreme care.

Lithium hypochlorite is a dry and stable compound commercially available at 35% available chlorine and has an alkaline pH. It is often used to super-chlorinate a pool. It also comes in dry granular compound and has high solubility. The disadvantages are high cost and relative short shelf-life at high temperatures. Lithium hypochlorite is a granular chlorinating compound with an active strength of 29 and an available chlorine content of 35. Its high solubility (43 grams per 100 grams of solution) and rapid dissolving rate is ideal for "super chlorination" of vinyl-lined and painted pools, as well as spas and hot tubs. Lithium hypochlorite is most commonly used as a "shocking" (super chlorination) agent, but has been successful as a primary sanitizer. As with other forms of chlorinating compounds, lithium hypochlorite reacts with water to produce hypochlorous acid (HOCl). Any increase in pH associated with its use is caused by the mildly alkaline byproduct, lithium hydroxide. Lithium hypochlorite's 29 active strength and 35 ACC is anomalous to other chlorinating compounds.

It is important to note that chlorine products are strong oxidizers. Chlorine products should never be mixed together or with other chemicals. Mixing chlorine products together may cause an explosion or fire. Mixing an acid with a chlorine product will result in the formation of deadly chlorine gas. All chemicals should be stored in its original, labeled packaging according to the manufacturer's instructions and the requirements of law.

BROMINE

Bromine is another disinfectant although not as popular as chlorine, it is worth mentioning. Bromine has several advantages over chlorine. It is an excellent disinfectant across wider range of pH than chlorine and does not produce an objectionable odor or eye irritation. However it is not widely used as chlorine since it is not a good oxidizer and it is usually more expensive.

Bromine must be dispensed in a device called a brominator which operates similar to an erosion-type chlorinator. Bromine levels in swimming pools should be kept between 3 - 5 ppm and 4 to 6 ppm in spas. Bromine in its elemental form is a reddish-brown liquid approximately three times heavier than water. It is extremely dangerous to handle. Safer forms of bromine have been developed such as Hydantoin bromine which come in sticks or tablets and can be used in an erosion-type feeder.

CHAPTER 4:
ROLE OF STABILIZERS
IN POOLS

There are two major classes of chlorinating agents: unstabilized (inorganic) and stabilized (organic).

Chlorine degrades rapidly in the sun. This is why you may need to service outdoor pool more often on sunny/hot day. In order to prevent chlorine from dissipating from sunlight, a stabilizer is used. This product attaches to and holds the chlorine until it is needed for disinfection.

The level of stabilizer in a pool should be maintained between 40 - 60 ppm. State law requires that it be kept below 100 ppm at all times in public pools. Frequent use of stabilized chlorine can lead to excessive levels of stabilizer. The only way to reduce the level of stabilizer is to partially drain and refill the pool. Stabilizer is slightly acidic and very slow in dissolving.

UNSTABILIZED CHLORINE

Unstabilized chlorine consists of chlorine gas (Cl_2), sodium hypochlorite (NaOCl), lithium hypochlorite (LiOCl), and calcium hypochlorite [$Ca(OCI)2$].

None of these unstabilized forms contain the atom, carbon (C), which is why they are also called inorganic chlorinating compounds. Organic molecules or compounds must contain carbon. Unstabilized chlorine is very sensitive to sunlight's ultraviolet (UV) radiation causing rapid available chlorine dissipation and reducing the water's disinfecting properties. Half of chlorine is removed from water every 30 minutes! On a warm sunny day 90% of chlorine dissipates in about 2 hours!

STABILIZED CHLORINE

As their name implies, stabilized chlorinating compounds are protected against the dissipative properties of sunlight. Before servicing any pool the process of picking correct chlorinating agent must be explored.

Even though state regulations allows 1.0-10.0 for the free-chlorine residual with stabilizer and 2.0-10.0 ppm using stabilizer; It is normal practice that free chlorine residuals in swimming pools be kept at 1.5-2.0 ppm without stabilizer and 2-2.5 ppm with stabilizer; spas, 2.0 – 3.0 ppm without stabilizer and 2.5 to 3.5 with stabilizer.

CYANURIC ACID AS A STABILIZER

Cyanuric acid (CYA) is a common additive that stabilizes chlorine in mostly outdoor swimming pools. Since sun is a major contributor to dissipative properties, it is not used as much at indoor swimming pool. Most of the stabilization is accomplished by the addition of cyanuric acid to the swimming pool. One of the main purpose of cyanuric acid is to reduce chlorine loss. This works because cyanuric acid has the unique ability to combine with chlorine to protect it against sunlight, it doesn't quite work the same way with bromine and it's ineffective. CYA dissolves slowly and lowers pH at the same time. As free available chlorine (FAC), the principle chlorine species responsible for disinfection and oxidation, is consumed, additional chlorine is released by cyanuric acid. Cyanuric acid has no disinfecting properties on its own; it is used exclusively as a chlorine stabilizer. However if not carefully monitored, the concentration can build to a point that exceeds to unsafe level and the only way to reduce CYA levels is to dilute it. Draining a portion of the pool water and refilling with fresh source water will reduce concentrations.

For maximum protection from the sun, cyanuric acid should be maintained between 40 - 60 ppm. Levels below 25 ppm are ineffective, and higher than recommended levels are not cost effective and even prohibited by some regulations. Keep in mind excessive levels of cyanuric acid can interfere with the disinfection.

TESTING OF CYANURIC ACID

Testing for cyanuric acid is most commonly done with a *turbidometric* test, which uses a test reagent to precipitate the cyanuric acid and then uses the relative cloudiness (turbidity) of the reacted sample to gauge the CYA concentration. A reagent called *melamine* is used. The melamine combines with the cyanuric acid in the water to form a fine, insoluble, white precipitate that causes the water to cloud in proportion to the amount of cyanuric acid in it. When the water clouds, it becomes more difficult to see an object in it. There also is an electronic test instrument (spectrophotometer) used to read the relative turbidity of the sample.

Some CYA test kits contain a specially designed vial, which has a black dot painted in the bottom of it that is clearly visible when it is filled with water but becomes more difficult to see when the CYA has been precipitated. How much of the dot you can see is compared to a chart included in the CYA test kit to indicate the concentration in ppm.

The newest method of CYA testing employs a dip-and-read test strip that is simply dipped into the pool water and changes color in about 30 seconds to indicate the level in ppm. High levels of cyanuric acid will cause a reduced ORP reading (read

OPR testing below). Manufacturers of ORP equipment recommend that a higher FAC be maintained to reach the desired 650 m V minimum. However for optimum protection, a 40 to 70 ppm cyanuric acid level should be maintained. Therefore, it is recommended that pools treated with unstabilized chlorine be initially "stabilized" to 50 ppm. Since stabilized chloroisocyanurates already contain cyanuric acid, their initial stabilizer level should be adjusted to 20 ppm. This is very important because trichlor and dichlor contain significant weight percentages of cyanuric acid. The maximum permissible cyanuric acid level is 100 ppm. There are also reports of algae growth and cloudy water with high cyanuric acid levels (100+ ppm). Therefore, proper stabilizer levels must exist for optimum product performance. Above 100+ does not provide additional stabilization and actually reduced disinfection and oxidation. Pool owners and operators should test for and maintain manufacturer's label recommended cyanuric acid levels to ensure optimum product performance.

TRICHLOR VS. DICHLOR

Stabilized Chlorine such as Trichloroisocyanuric Acid and Sodium Dichloroisocyanuric Acid are two primary forms of stabilized chlorine used for pool and spa application.

Although frequently used in indoor pools, trichlor's stabilization characteristics make it ideal for outdoor pool use; indoor pool environments lack sunlight, eliminating the need for stabilization or stabilized chlorinating agents. Trichloroisocyanuric has about 89 % free available chlorine, it lowers pH of pool water. It comes in dry tablet, sticks or granules, it dissolves very slowly and due to this it's not used to super-chlorinate. As with other pool/spa oxidizers, trichlor requires special handling and care must be exercised when using this chlorinating agent. It is available in a variety of physical configurations ranging from 1" tablets to 1 pound sticks.

Sodium dichlor's increased rate of dissolution and relatively neutral pH is favored by many pool and spa. Dichlor has about 62 % free available chlorine and its pH is close to neutral. It also contains cyanuric acid but it can be used to super chlorinate a pool. Dichlor cannot be stabilized like its chlorine counterpart, trichlor. Therefore, dichlor is available in granular form only. Its high solubility permits direct application to the pool or spa.

The major difference between dichlor and trichlor is the number of chlorine atoms and the presence of sodium (Na) in dichlor. The subsequent production of sodium hydroxide is what gives dichlor its neutral pH. As previously mentioned, cyanuric acid constitutes a major weight; this large cyanuric acid weight percentage and dichlor's ease of application can cause a quick rise in stabilizer levels. Many customers who use dichlor as a primary sanitizer also use it as a shocking agent. This will magnify the problem. Therefore, pool owners using dichlor as a primary sanitizer should use an unstabilized form of chlorine for shocking purposes.

CHAPTER 5:
WATER BALANCE

In addition to having proper disinfection and the role of chlorine in the pool, you will also have to consider other aspect of balanced water. Water balance is the relationship of pool chemicals in the water. You will have to learn to control other water behavior that can lead to corrosive such as scale forming attributes, oxidation, removal of organic debris and changing elements from soluble to insoluble state. The ideal pool water provides a comfortable environment for the swimmer while resisting the growth of pathogens, algae and other organisms. The other factors to consider are temperature, pH, total alkalinity, total hardness, and total dissolved solids (TDS) and Langlier Saturation index.

PH

The pH of pool water is a measurement of its acidity or alkalinity or measurement of its hydrogen ion content. The pH scale means "the potential for hydrogen", and is a measurement of hydrogen ion [H+], thus measuring its acidity or alkalinity in any substance. An increase in [H+] ion lowers pH and increases acidity. Decrease in [H+] ion increases pH and make the water more basic. The pH range can extend from 0 to 14. At a pH of 7 the water is neutral, neither acidic nor basic. As the pH is lowered towards 1, the water becomes more acidic. As the pH is raised towards 14, the water becomes more basic or alkaline. Each unit represents a tenfold increase or decrease in acidity, so a pH of 3 is 10 x more acidic than a pH of 4 and a pH of 2 is 1,000 x more acidic than a pH of 5. The regulation requires that the pH in a public pool be kept between 7.2 and 8.0. The pH of pool water should be kept between 7.4 and 7.6 for more comfortable environment for bathers. Acidic pool water can cause damage to pool equipment and high levels may injure swimmers. As the pH is raised from 7 to 14, the more alkaline it becomes. Alkaline pool water can cause itchy skin and eyes and cloudy water. At pH 7.0, swimming pool water is neutral, neither acidic nor alkaline (basic). Most pool's pH for effective disinfection using chlorine should be kept between 7.4 and 7.6. However pH between 7.2-7.8, not ideal but may suffice. Chlorine disinfects more efficiently at this range of pH. The acidity and alkalinity of swimming pool water can also affect the growth of algae and other organisms. It is important to maintain the pH at proper ranges because it also regulates effectiveness of chlorine as a disinfectant.

THE EFFECT OF DISINFECTANTS ON PH

Liquid Chlorine (sodium hypochlorite)	Raises pH
Trichlor	Lowers pH
Dichlor	Lowers pH
Lithium Hypochlorite	Raises pH
Gas chlorine	Lowers pH

The pH of pool water is normally measured using a chemical called Phenol Red. A drop or two of Sodium Thiosulfate is also added to the test before the Phenol Red to eliminate any residual chlorine which will interfere with the test. The dropper bottle should be held in a vertical position when dispensing the drops and the hand should not be used to cover the test vial when mixing as this may produce false readings. Various chemicals are used to adjust the pH which is raised or lowered by makeup water or the addition of chlorine products (See above one which chlorine raises/lowers pH):

CHEMICALS THAT RAISES PH

Soda ash (Sodium Carbonate) is used to raise the pH of pool water. It comes in a powdered form and is broadcasted directly into the pool.

Caustic soda (Sodium Hydroxide) is a highly corrosive liquid which is also used to raise the pH usually in larger pools. It is pumped into the recirculation system at a controlled rate using a displacement pump.

Baking soda (Sodium Bicarbonate) is used to raise the total alkalinity and not appreciably change the pH.

CHEMICALS THAT LOWERS PH

Muriatic acid (Hydrochloric Acid) is used to lower the pH of pool water as well as dry acid (Sodium Bisulfate-NaHSO4). No more than one half quart of liquid acid per 10,000 gallons should be added at one time to a pool. One hour should be allowed between half quart doses. One should never refill any empty chemical containers with a chemical other than the same chemical that originally came in that container.

Acid should be poured into the deep end of the pool and not into the skimmer or shallow end. Excessive acid in a pool can cause blue staining by leaching copper from the recirculation piping and heat exchanger. When pool water has been in an acidic state for an extended period of time, the water should be checked for copper levels over 0.2 ppm before adjusting the pH or else blue staining from the formation of copper carbonate can occur. The only solution for high copper levels is to drain or partially drain the pool and refill to lower the copper level.

TOTAL ALKALINITY

Total alkalinity greatly influences where the pH will stabilize to after a pH adjusting chemical is used. Total alkalinity is basically a pH stabilizer. Total alkalinity is the level of bicarbonate, carbonate and hydroxide alkalinity in the water. It is a measure of a given amount of water that is buffered. The amounts depend on the pH of the pool. At the normal pH It usually acts as a buffer in water to protect against pH change. Total alkalinity should be maintained between 80 - 150 ppm in plaster pools and 125 - 175 ppm in non-plaster type pools.

Low alkalinity will have pH bounce all over the place, it can also contribute to causing green water and plaster etching. It is likely to cause corrosion (metal parts, copper in heater, copper pipes). Sodium bicarbonate (baking soda) is used to raise the total alkalinity but won't noticeably change the pH.

High alkalinity causes cloudy water, hard to adjust pH down. Commonly muriatic acid or sodium bisulfate is used to lower alkalinity.

Testing for total alkalinity is essential to making proper determinations of the saturation index (discussed later) as well as bather comfort and for pH control. Total alkalinity should be considered before adjusting pH. The direction of pH change, or even the need for adding chemicals, is greatly influenced by the level of total alkalinity. Total alkalinity does not vary quickly and often is only tested once a week. At normal pH, most of the alkalinity is in the form of bicarbonate alkalinity.

TOTAL HARDNESS

Total hardness is a measure of the amount of mineral content of water (calcium, magnesium and other metal ions in water). Total hardness and calcium hardness can be determined independently, as described below. Hard water mostly refers to water that is high in calcium, high surface tension, decreased ability to form foam or suds. On the other hand soft water is just the opposite, water that is low in calcium, has low surface tensions and readily foams. Low calcium water generally causes plaster etching and corrosion. To raise hardness, mostly calcium chloride is used and maintained between 200-300ppm. In source water, the content is often 65 to 75 of the total, with the remainder primarily magnesium. In pool water especially if it has been in the pool for any length of time 90 to 95 of the hardness is due to calcium. Total hardness is the most important consideration in pool water mineral content, although you may wish to test specifically for calcium hardness if the pool has been recently filled. The calcium hardness level in pool water should be kept between 200 and 300 ppm.

High calcium levels may lead to the formation of calcium carbonate (scale), which results in rough plaster surfaces, clogged pipes, reduced circulation, heater inefficiency, and eye irritation. It also causes rough pool surface, filter calcification. To correct high calcium levels, the pool should be partially drained and refilled. Sometimes water softeners are used and sequestering agent are used to hold calcium in solution.

Low calcium levels can result in etching and pitting of plaster, and corrosive water. To correct low calcium levels add calcium chloride to the pool water. Low calcium hardness is usually not a problem on the west coast as hard water is usually replenished by make-up water into the pool.

Calcium hardness in a freshly filled pool can be approximated by taking 70 of the total hardness level. However, more accurate measurements can be made by using a test kit designed specifically to determine calcium hardness and by following the manufacturer's directions regarding color changes. In these tests, a specific amount of water is taken from the pool, and an indicator is added to the sample. A reagent is added, causing a color change that indicates the calcium hardness level in ppm.

TOTAL DISSOLVED SOLIDS (TDS)

Another indication of water quality is the level of total dissolved solids (TDS) in the water. Total dissolved solids (TDS) is the measurement of electrochemical measurement of water to conduct an electrical current (charged particles in water ions). This depends on all materials dissolved in the water, i.e., calcium, carbonates, dissolved organic and inorganic materials and salts from chlorine residue. Swimmer's waste, soluble hair, body lotion or any other waste placed in the pool that can be dissolved.

High TDS around 1,500 ppm above water-supply level can reduce chlorine efficiency by as much as 50 and can cause electrical current. High TDS water tastes salty and offers a dull appearance. High TDS is common with spa water with high bather load and a relatively small volume of water. Outdoor pools exposed to lots of sun maybe subject to high TDS due to evaporation, more prevalent in pools that are shallow with low volume of water.

TDS can only be corrected by dilution of water with low TDS. Pools/spas are usually drained and diluted with water that has low TDS. A pool should be dumped and refilled when a TDS reading exceeds 1,500 ppm above the domestic water supply reading. TDS is measured by using a portable electronic analyzer. The equipment is specifically used to measure for dissolved solids. Neutral particles are not measured as TDS, only the charged particles are measured.

High TDS can cause algae growth despite adequate chlorine residuals and interference with disinfectants. High TDS can also cause cloudy water despite good filtration and chlorination, false readings on chlorine tests, and eye and skin irritation.

CHAPTER 6:
TESTING THE WATER

Before you begin testing chemical, take all safety precautions. Chemical safety is important! You should never mix chemicals, always add chemical to water, never add water to chemical. Follow all instructions. Use eye and skin protection when needed. Store chemicals in a safe, cool, dry area and discard all hazardous chemical properly.

Daily testing for the level of disinfectant in public pool water is required. However your basic pool testing kit should also measure pH, total alkalinity, calcium hardness, TDS and stabilizers. These tests are usually colorimetric (reaction causing change in color) test were you will need to compare color obtained in water to standard color chart.

It is important to carefully follow the manufacturer's directions supplied with the kit. The pool water sample should be taken between 12 to 18 inches below the surface of the water. After testing, don't return the test sample back into the pool.

ORTHOTOLIDINE/DPD TEST

Orthotolidine is a common chemical used to test for chlorine residual. Its disadvantage is that it cannot accurately measure both free and combined chlorine. DPD type test kits on the other hand, can measure both free and combined chlorine levels and are the only type that can be used at commercial pools. You should remember from our earlier examples that the combined chlorine residual can be calculated by subtracting the free chlorine residual from the total chlorine residual. Water for testing should be taken from 12 to 18 inches below the surface of the water. Orthotolidine or DPD tablets should never be dropped directly into the water as the results will be inaccurate and introduction of the chemicals in the water could be harmful. Water from tests should not be thrown back into the pool. Directions which come with the kit should be carefully followed.

DPD test kits or a test kit that is capable of testing free-halogen residual may be used in public pools. It is important to note that high halogen levels may cause inaccurate results for the DPD test kit and determination of pH and total alkalinity.

DPD type chlorine test kit, first a #1 tablet is added to measure the amount of free chlorine that is in the water. A #3 tablet is then added to the water to measure the total chlorine in the water. To calculate the combined chlorine, one must subtract the free chlorine reading from the total chlorine reading. If you are using bromine residual multiply the free chlorine reading by 2.25.

General reading on your testing for chlorine without stabilizer should be 1.0PPM, if stabilizer is used minimum should at least be around 1.5PPM.

Bromine reading should be around 2.25PPM. As we mentioned ideal pH should be around 7.4-7.6, even though you can probably get away with 7.2-8.0.

Cyanuric acid's ideal range around 25-100PPM, however if you are concerned about the cost factor you can also get away with having it around 40PPM.

TESTING FOR ALKALINITY

A pool's total alkalinity may be determined through use of many commercially available test kits. Since there are many reagents used, it's hard to know the procedure for everyone. Basically a quantity of pool water is mixed with an indicator; a specific color reveals the presence of alkalinity, a reagent is added to this mixture from a dropper. The operator counts the number of drops necessary to neutralize the alkalinity and bring about a color change. Alkalinity can be determined by multiplying the number of drops used by a constant as provided by the test kit manufacturer (usually 1 drop = 10 ppm).

Tablet methods also are available for determining alkalinity. Although less accurate than the drop counting method, the process is easy to follow and is less susceptible to operator error. Tablets are added one at a time until the desired color change takes place. When sufficient tablets have been added to bring about the end-point color change, the number of tablets required is multiplied by the constant provided by the test-kit manufacturer.

TESTING FOR HARDNESS

To test for total hardness, a specific amount of pool water is treated with a solution called a buffer. Then a dye is added. The reagent is added to the sample and mixed, one drop at a time. The number of drops necessary to change the water color, multiplied by a constant provided by the manufacturer, the tablet method for testing water hardness is equally simple. A tablet containing the pH buffer, the indicator dye, and the hardness reagent is added to a 100 ml sample of water. The color changes as additional tablets are added. The number of tablets required to bring about this change is recorded and multiplied by a constant provided by the test-kit manufacturer. However, test kits are actually only measuring calcium hardness. Calcium chloride should be added to establish more normal calcium hardness levels.

TESTING FOR IRON

Iron in low concentration also can be measured with readily available test kits. The standard test for iron is a straight colorimetric test using an indicator reagent, available in both liquid form and in premeasured "powder pillows." When added to the test sample, the reagent reacts with iron to produce varying shades of orange-red, which then can be compared to a color standard provided by the manufacturer to determine iron concentration.

ORP-OXIDATION REDUCTION PRINCIPAL

Testing method which considers oxidation testing is ORP. The oxidation reduction potential (ORP) is an effective measure of the oxidizing properties of any sanitizer being used in a pool or spa and is measured in millivolts (m V). ORP measuring chemical controllers are used for automating the additions of chlorine or sanitizers and pH balancers (acids or alkaline) in an effort to maintain predetermined chemical parameters. These properties are determined by a sensor of a noble metal electrode, usually platinum, and a standard silver/silver chloride reference electrode. An ORP sensor acts like a small battery that creates a small, measurable electric potential. ORP can vary over a wide range from a few m V to 800 m V or more. In 1972, the World Health Organization accepted the standard of 650 m V as the level for the treatment of drinking water. It was found that water at this level is disinfected, and viral inactivation is almost instantaneous. In 1982, an ORP of 750 m V was accepted by Germany and some European countries as a minimum health standard for swimming pools, and the same ORP was accepted for spas in 1984.In the United States, it is the recommendation of the pool and spa industry that 650 m V be the minimum standard and 750 mV the preferred. ORP is a measure of the oxidizing power of any sanitizer in water. When used with chlorine, an ORP sensor measures primarily the level of hypochlorous acid (HOCl) as it disassociates according to pH (Table 5.1, p. 32) in pool or spa: water.

THE SATURATION INDEX OR LANGLIER INDEX

The Saturation Index (Langelier Index) is a scale that indicates if pool water has scaling or etching properties. It is used to measure corrosiveness or scaling tendencies of pool water. The factors in determining langlier index include pH, water temperature, total alkalinity, and calcium hardness. The values of these factors are taken from the table, totaled and the TDS value is subtracted to arrive at the saturation index. A saturation index of 0 indicates the water is balanced. A negative number greater than -0.5 indicates the water may be corrosive to metals in the pool and may etch the pool plaster. A number greater than +0.5 indicates the water may form calcium deposits clogging recirculation pipes and filter grids, and may stain pool plaster. Pool test results for water balance factors are used in saturation index formula. Special factor is assigned to alkalinity, calcium and temperature.

CHAPTER 7:
POOL RECIRCULATORY EQUIPMENT

The recirculation system of a pool is nothing more than set of equipment that recycles, filters and adds a disinfectant to the water prior to returning back to the pool. It consists of a main drain (that must be unblockable, a drain of any size and shape that a human body cannot sufficiently block to create a suction entrapment hazard to comply with Virginia Graeme Baker) and skimmer where the water is drawn to a pump which forces the water through a filter and a heater and returns back to the pool through several return lines.

Typical commercial pool recirculation system works this way:

Pool water → Drawn in through main drain and skimmer → Into the pump → Filtered → Monitored by flowmeter → Heater (optional) → Chlorine/other disinfectant is added via chlorinator → Returned back to the pool

Note: Spa will have boosters for jets as well

Pumps, filters, and all related parts of a public pool recirculation system must be kept in operation whenever the pool or spa is available for use and as long as necessary to maintain the water in a clean and clear condition. This usually requires 20 - 24 hours a day for a public pool. Pools should never be used if the water becomes so cloudy that the main drain is not clearly visible from any part of the deck. Pool recirculation system shall be in operation whenever the pool or spa is in use. "In use" means whenever the spa/pool is open for use, does not matter if there are any active swimmers present or not. Recirculation system should be in use as long as necessary to maintain the water in a clean and clear condition. Unless the recirculation system is continually on, time clocks for the pool recirculation system and lights should be properly set.

TURNOVER RATE

The recirculation system continuously removes water from the pool, filters and disinfects the water and returns the clean water back to the pool. The amount of water being filtered (flow rate, which is monitored by flowmeter) is expressed in gallons per minute (GPM).

The length of time it takes to filter a volume of water equivalent to the volume of water in the pool is called the turnover time. The required turnover time for a public swimming pool is 6 hours or less. Public spas shall have a turnover time of one half hour or less. Public wading pools shall have a turnover time of 1 hour or less.

Calculate turnover time:

To calculate the flow rate required for a 36,000 gallon swimming pool

Divide 36,000 by 6 hours multiplied by 60 minutes (36,000 / 60 x 6).

In this example the flow rate is 100 gallons per minute.

This means if a 36,000 gallon pool has a flow rate of 100 gpm, it would have a turnover time of 6 hours or (36,000/100 x 60).

We will cover more calculations later. At this time, know what turnover time should be and how to calculate turnover time.

POOL EQUIPMENT

PUMPS

The pump pushes water through the recirculation system. Pumps are comprised of impeller, wheel-like device that rotates and slings water outward and volute, a housing chamber for impeller. Size of the pump depends on the size/volume of the pool

Pump must put out enough flow to achieve the required turnover time. Recirculation system must run whenever the pool is open for use and longer if necessary to keep the water clear. This is done by creating a vacuum which circulates pool water.

The most common type of recirculation pump used on pools is the centrifugal pump. The term total dynamic head in a recirculating system is the measurement of the resistance of the water flowing through pipes and equipment. Pumps are rated in horsepower and are sized using pump curves. A pump curve is a chart showing the various flow rates at different "feet of head". The greater the "feet of head" the less water flows. The shut-off head is the "feet of head" at which there is no flow. In a recirculation system, total dynamic head can be measured by placing a vacuum gauge on the suction side of the pump and a pressure gauge on the discharge side. The readings are converted to pounds per square inch and added together.

If a pump is operated without enough water being supplied on the suction side, cavitation occurs. Cavitation is defined as the formation of vapor bubbles within a liquid at low-pressure regions that occur in places where the liquid has been accelerated to high velocities. Cavitation can be identified by a rumbling noise, air bubbles at the discharge pipe and erratic pressure gauge and flowmeter readings. Cavitation causes damage to the impeller and can impair or destroy the pump. This can result in a significant reduction of efficiency because the flow pattern is distorted.

The maximum velocity in the pump suction hydraulic system shall not exceed six feet per second when 100 percent of the pump's flow comes from the main drain system and any main drain suction fitting in the system is completely blocked.

SKIMMER/SKIMMING PROCESS

Skimmer is a device installed in the wall of a pool to pull in water and floating contaminants. Floating particulates are skimmed from the surface of the water. Small percentage of water is actually recirculated via skimmer; most of the water goes through the main drain.

The weir or flapper or donut ring type of weir on a skimmer is required to provide for proper skimming of the surface of the water. The weir (flapper or ring) on a skimmer is necessary to provide proper skimming of the surface of the water, without a weir, skimming doesn't occur. An anti-air lock device within the skimmer prevents air from entering the suction line if the water level drops below the skimmer opening. Skimmer baskets should be cleaned on a regular basis and replaced when broken. Skimmers not connected to the main drain are required to have an equalizer line located below the skimmer opening. The equalizer line prevents air from entering the suction line if the water level gets too low. Skimmers with an equalizer line should have an equalizer valve installed inside the skimmer. This valve normally remains closed allowing full skimming, but opens when the water level is low. Perimeter overflow pools or rim flow skimming systems flow to a surge chamber and are mainly used on larger pools. The surge chamber is used to balance the level of water in the pool and maintain skimming even when large numbers of people enter the pool.

Skimmer related parts

Weir - draws water into the skimmer.

Basket - collects large debris.

Air Lock Device - prevents air suction into pump.

Diverter Valve - regulates flow from main drain.

Skimmer Equalizer Line - a suction outlet located below the waterline and connected to the body of a skimmer that prevents air from being drawn into the pump if the water level drops below the skimmer weir. It ensures water is provided to pump.

AUTOMATIC DISINFECTANT FEEDER

Automatic disinfectant feeders continually dispense a small amount of disinfectant into the recirculation system. Automatic chlorinators are the most common disinfectant feeders. Automatic chlorinators are commonly available as a positive displacement type pump which utilizes a reservoir, or an erosion-type feeder. A positive displacement pump is connected to a timer which pumps the liquid solution directly into the recirculation system. Erosion-type chlorinators are attached to the recirculation system at two points with different pressure levels. This cause's recirculation water to flow into the chlorinator past chlorine tablets with slowly dissolves and introduces the chlorine product into the recirculation system. Similarly a Bromine tablets or sticks in an erosion-type feeder are called a brominator.

All public pools are required to have an automatic chlorinator. Manual dispensing is not in place of automatic disinfection is not allowed, neither are floating type chlorinators or tablets placed in skimmers. Chlorinators should be periodically taken apart and cleaned with dilute Muriatic Acid. Automatic Chlorinators are required on all commercial pools/spas, not residential pools.

They must be capable of producing 2 lbs. of pure chlorine or 10,000 gallons/day.

EXAMPLE:

60,000 GALLON POOL

2 LBS. CHLORINE X 60,000= 2 LBS. x 6
10,000
= 12 LBS. OF CHLORINE / DAY

There are many different types of chlorinators on the market:

Liquid (hypochlorinator) are chemical feed pump (positive displacement pump). Pump and feed lines cleaned with dilute acid.

Dry chlorinator holds dry chlorine products (tablets, sticks, granules). Water enters chlorinator and dissolves dry chlorine product.

Chlorine (salt) generators chlorinator where salt is added to the pool and chlorine is generated by electrical current.

Gas chlorinators are rarely used due to safety issues. Erosion factors and solubility of the product should be considered.

Best injection point for all chlorinators is after the heater.

FILTERS

A swimming pool filter removes suspended particles in the form of organisms, hair, skin, and other particles from the water. Filter must be sized to handle the turnover rate. There are various types of filters on the market and as technology improves more may come on the market.

As of today most common type of filters used are Diatomaceous Earth (D.E.), Rapid Sand, High Rate Sand and Cartridge filters.

DE filters do the best job of filtering pool water, high rate and rapid sand the next best, and cartridge filters the least. Let's discuss them in more detail.

DIATOMACEOUS EARTH (DE) FILTER

Diatomaceous earth filters are the most common type of filters used on pools, especially in Southern California. They consist of a plastic frame covered with a cloth element. Diatomaceous earth is a white powder, when added in the skimmer, coats these cloth elements. Diatomaceous earth is made up of the fossil remains of tiny aquatic plants called diatoms. It is the DE that traps the dirt and debris, not the cloth elements. They are designed with filter grids, made up of plastic frame and synthetic bag which fits over the frame. Filter rating is about 2 GPM/sq. ft. DE sticks to bag and does the filtering. It can remove particles 1 micron in size.

A DE filter should never be used without diatomaceous earth or dirt will clog the cloth elements. If this happens scrub the elements with a non-foaming detergent. The effective area of filters is measured in square feet. The usual amount of earth added to a DE filter is about one half pound per 5 square feet of filter area. DE filters to be sized at not more than 2 gallons per minute per square foot. This means that a 30 sq. ft. filter can have a maximum of 60 gallons per minute flowing through it. A slightly oversized filter will give you a longer filter run between backwashes

Filters are cleaned by backwashing. This is accomplished by reversing the flow of water through the filter using a combination of valves or a multiport valve, and flushing the DE along with accumulated dirt to a waste container. Some cities require DE waste to be routed to a separation tank and then to a sanitary sewer or other approved disposal system. From time to time, the filter should be disassembled for a more thorough cleaning. Oils and grease can be removed from filter elements with a non-foaming type detergent. Scale can be removed by using diluted muriatic acid. The larger the effective area, the longer the filter can run without requiring backwashing. There are two pressure gauges at most public pools. The one on top of the filter is the influent pressure gauge and the one after the filter is the effluent pressure gauge. The correct pressure reading is the influent minus the effluent reading. Starting pressures on clean filters will vary with different systems. When the pressure gauge reading indicates that the pressure has increased approximately 10 psi over the starting pressure, it is time to backwash the filter. Filter grids are usually removed 2 to 3 times a year. You should inspect them for torn fabric, oil or scale deposits. You can clean this by using soaking solution (tri-sodium phosphate). If you find the filter high in scale deposit, soak grid in dilute acid solution (10 parts water to 1 part muriatic acid). Always remove oil deposits first.

Potential problems with DE filter range from air accumulation in filter (which must be removed by air release valve), Bridging (Filter grids too close together), gap between grids becomes sealed (loss of filter area), It should be maintained at least 1" apart. Clean filter has unusually high pressure reading; possible scale deposits on filter media or filter grid, you can correct this by soaking grid in diluted acid solution. If the filter is allowed to operate without DE in it, it can cause oil deposits on filter grid, this can be corrected by soaking grid in detergent solution or replacing grids or by adding DE.

You can also pre-coat the filter by adding new DE to filter (Add 2 oz. DE / Sq. Ft. of filter surface area), Add DE through skimmer.

Example:

Amount of DE to pre-coat a 48 sq. ft. filter:

2 oz. DE x 48 sq. ft. = 96 oz. of DE (6 Ibs.).

RAPID SAND & HIGH RATE SAND FILTER

These types of filters use varying grades of sand for filtering. As water passes through the layers of sand, contaminates are removed. Most of the filtration occurs on the surface of the sand.

High rate sand filter's rating is 15-20 GPM/sq. ft. Filtering is done through entire depth of sand bed and does not use filter aid. The flow through high rate sand filters is much faster than rapid sand filters and consequently is much smaller in size.

High rate sand filter are sized at 15 gallons per minute per square foot.

Rapid sand filter's rating is 3 GPM/sq.ft. Backwash is done at 10 differentials on pressure gauges. Filter aid (coagulant, flocculent) joins small colloidal particles together (forms floc). Alum (aluminum sulfate) is a popular filter aid. Filtering occurs in top portions of sand bed. These filters are backwashed using the same methods as in DE filters. Water is flushed backwards through the sand filter to a waste container. Backwash water should never be returned to the pool. Rapid sand filters are used on large municipal pools and are much larger than high rate sand filters. Rapid sand filters are sized at 3 gallons per minute per square foot.

To aid in filtration flocculants and coagulants principal are also used. These chemical products used are used in pool water to combine small particles of dirt. The larger particles can then be more easily filtered from the pool. Aluminum sulfate (Alum) is a flocculent often added in pools utilizing rapid sand filters. With the proper pH and alkalinity the alum will form a gelatinous floc which will stick to the sand. Particles will then become trapped in the floc.

CARTRIDGE FILTER

Cartridge filters are made of a pleated cloth element. As water passes through the cartridge dirt and debris are trapped in fabric. Filter media is made of synthetic material. Cartridge filters are comprised of air relief valve, lower manifold, and a bulkhead.

Dirt is trapped on the elements as the water is forced through the filter. When dirty, cartridge filters are taken out of the filter holder and hosed down, scrubbed and disinfected in a chlorine solution. Cartridge are dried and returned to the filter. Cartridge filters should be allowed to completely dry before being put back into service. These filters must be disassembled each time the filter needs cleaning. Additional set of filter elements shall be available for installation while the existing filter elements are cleaned. Cartridge filters are sized at 0.375 gallons per minute per square foot, which make it least effective in filtering water.

PRESSURE GAUGES

Typically two pressure gauges were required for each filter; however recent change in regulations may only require one gauge. Influent Gauge measures incoming water pressure and effluent gauge measures outgoing water pressure. To be accurate both gauges should be at the same elevation. Influent gauge is placed after the pump and before the filter and effluent gauge is placed after the filter. As mentioned above, differential in pressure is used to determine if the filter needs cleaning.

SEPARATION TANK

Separation Tank collects D.E. or sand from backwash water. An air gap (2 x pipe diameter) is required between the discharge pipe and sewer drain.

SIGHT GLASS

Sight glass is a clear section of backwash pipe between filter and separation tank, it is used to observe clarity of backwash water. A sight glass is used predominately to observe the dirty water when backwashing the filter. When the water is clear the backwashing is complete. Frequently a sight glass is not needed because backwash water can be observed at the air-gap between the backwash line and p-trap.

FLOWMETER

A flow meter is a device that indicates the rate of flow of a recirculation system in gallons per minute. Flowmeters are required on all public pools. On small pools, the meter is usually plastic tubes with an indicator weight. On large pools it may be a mechanical gauge resembling an rpm meter on a car. Flow meters are usually installed after the filter to prevent clogging. Best location to place flowmeter is after the filter and before the heater on a straight run of horizontal pipe. If space is available would be 10 pipe diameters in length of straight pipe before flowmeter and 4 pipe diameters in length of straight pipe after flowmeter. The flow meter should also be located far enough away from the heater to prevent warping.

CHAPTER 8:
PLUMBING

The plumbing for newly constructed pools shall have the capacity to provide a complete turnover of pool water within 6hrs or less; One-half hour or less for a spa pool; One-half hour or less for a spray ground; One-half hour or less for a wading pool; Two hours or less for a medical pool.

Piping must be constructed and designed to handle the flow. It must be sized according to flow rate, maximum allowable flow rate are:

PVC pipe 8 ft./sec in Suction Lines

PVC pipe 10 ft./sec in Return Lines

Copper pipe 8 ft./sec in Suction or Return Lines

The water velocity in all suction line plumbing shall not exceed 6 feet per second and in all return lines water velocity shall not exceed 8 feet per second. Previously, it was 8 feet per second for suction lines and 10 feet per second for return lines.

This does not apply to existing pools unless the entire suction or return plumbing is being replaced. For newly constructed pools exceeding 40 ft. in width, or greater than 3,000 sq. ft. in surface area, bottom floor return lines are required. Previously, only pools greater than 40 ft. in width required bottom floor return lines. An influent pressure gauge before each filter and a vacuum gauge before each pump is also required.

Make-up water for a pool shall be from a potable source. The fill line shall have the proper type of backflow protection. Backflow protection prevents the water from the pool from being drawn back into the public water supply or other potable water source.

For fill lines directly connected to the recirculation system and under pressure, a reduced pressure principle backflow device must be used.

BACKFLOW DEVICE

Atmospheric Vacuum Breaker (anti-siphon device) - used when no valves are downstream from the main valve.

Pressure Vacuum Breaker - used when there is downstream valving.

Reduced Pressure Principal Backflow Device - used when the fill line is connected to a pressurized line.

Hose bibs require an atmospheric vacuum breaker.

Another method of backflow prevention is a space between two devices called an air-gap. An air-gap is often used on the back wash line connection to the sanitary sewer line to prevent the sewer liquids from entering the pool water.

CHAPTER 9:
OZONE

Ozone is an unstable gas that must be produced on site. Ozone use in swimming pool is not that common. However if you encounter a pool that uses ozone, you should be familiar with the basics.

Ozone must be used with either bromine or chlorine. Ozone is produced using either ultraviolet or corona discharge; it is a strong disinfectant and an oxidizer and doesn't affect the pH.

When you are using ozone in a pool it's important to keep in mind some of the requirements. You must keep free halogen residual in the pool; equipment must only be used to augment the required free halogen residual. Ozone generating cleaning and maintenance of equipment should be accessible and should be capable of alerting the operator when a component of the equipment is not operating. Ozone generating equipment should be equipped with an air flow meter that has check valve between the ozone generator and the injection point(to be located in the pool return line after the filtration and heating equipment, prior to the disinfectant injection point and a minimum of 10 feet from the nearest pool return inlet).

It is also important not to have any other chemicals where ozone equipment are present, especially any solvents or any combustible materials other than those required for the operation of the pool recirculation and ozone generating equipment. In case of emergency a standard operating procedure manual containing information on the operation and maintenance of the ozone generating equipment should also be present.

If ozone generating equipment is located indoors, different set of rules apply. First you must make sure there is ample of ventilation (3 air changes per hour), and in emergency situation and ventilation should be able to pick up the air change to up to 30 air changes/per hour. An audio and visual ozone detection/alarm system should be located in the room containing the ozone generating equipment.

It is also important that if needed ozone generating equipment can be automatically shut off when there is a loss of electrical power to the pool, recirculation pump or the ozone booster pump. Additionally automatic shut off should also shut off if intake air flow falls below manufacturer's operational minimums, Ozone generator door or panel is open or if there is a leaks or failure of the oxygen generation equipment.

Ozone should also be tested using dragger tube or other device to make sure concentrations of ozone in the air space within 6 inches of the pool water level does not exceed 0.1 ppm above the air ozone concentration. This test should be done at minimum at the time ozone generating equipment is installed and annually thereafter.

CHAPTER 10:
GROW YOUR BUSINESS EXPONENTIALLY!

If you have your own pool business and are familiar with swimming pool codes you can recommend a lot more service to your clients. Most pool technicians service the pool water and leave. Servicing water usually mostly means checking free chlorine residual (1.0 ppm and 1.5ppm when cyanuric acid is used), maintaining proper pH (between 7.2 and 8.0), stocking up chlorine, backwashing if needed, brushing dirty tiles and raking in/vacuuming pool from leaves and particulates, cleaning algae growth in the pool, etc....

However if you or your service technician know some of the codes you can generate a lot more income and ensure that your clients are in compliance with the state regulations. Your aim is grab a lot bigger piece of the pie for fraction of the time.

First and very important thing to understand is these codes only apply to commercial pool, not residential pool. Commercial or public pools are not private resident pools. They include pools found in small hotels, motels, bigger hotel/motels, water parks, fitness center, private clubs, motor home parks, etc...

Most pools have a lot more deficiencies than just adjusting pool water. You will find some form of pool code violation 90% of the time.

You or your service technician is there to service the pool and I want them to literally take 5 minutes more for big potential profits.

I have included basic pool code violations below backed by law!

1. I would like your company to create a template inspection report with check off list, create multiple copies and pass it out to your service technicians.

2. This check off list should have your company logo and sited violation code (which I have provided for you below) next to the violation you are citing.

3. Once your tech. has finished servicing the swimming pool, have them spend 5 mins, scanning the pool area and fill off a checking of the list.

4. Once you have cited the violation backed by law send this inspection report along with your invoice to your client as complimentary inspection that you have provided to bring them into compliance with state law.

5. To generate money:

   a. Small repairs can be done by your company.

   b. Missing signs can be provided by you.

   c. However most pool companies are not in the business of fixing pool items, thus you need to create a referral program. Reach out to pool contractors and sign vendors and work out a referral program. You can have third party do major construction work for small referral fee.

I find offering small services for free, helps to build credibility and on personal level it's not just about milking people for every penny but offering good service. These services are rarely offered.

UNDERSTANDING POOL CODES

Let's review some of the common/easy violations that exist at swimming pools. Again create a check off list of these items. I have created the requirement in plain English and then have cited codes at the end of the book.

DEPTH MARKERS

Depth markers numerals must be at least 4 inches in height. Permanent depth markers are required on the pool deck, corresponding to every depth marker on the wall. All depth markers must be marked with the letters "Feet" or "Ft." and "Inches" or "In".

Painted or stick-on numbers are not permitted. Rim flow pools can have depth markers installed below the waterline.

For pools with a maximum water depth of 6 ft. or less, permanent "no diving" markers (tiles) are required next to each of the deck depth markers.

For spa pools, two "no diving" markers are required. For existing pools, depth markers on the deck and "no diving" markers on the deck are required when the deck is replaced or resurfaced. The remaining depth marker requirements are required when the depth markers or water line tiles are replaced.

STAIRS

All stairs must be at least 24 in. wide. All risers must be no greater than 12 inches high. The top riser is considered that distance from the deck or coping down to the first tread of the stair and the deck. The first tread below the deck must be at least 14 inches but not greater than 18 inches wide. The remaining treads must be 12 inches but not greater than 16 inches wide. If the top tread is convexly or triangularly shaped, it must have a radius of a minimum of 21 inches but not greater than 24inches. All treads except for the top tread must be uniform.

HANDRAIL

The height of handrails must be between 28 inches and 36 inches. Spas are required to have two handrails regardless of riser height. For existing pools: when pools are re-plastered or resurfaced, handrails must comply with the new handrail requirements. Regardless of step heights, spas will be required to have two handrails when the spa is' re-plastered or resurfaced.

POOL EQUIPMENT REQUIREMENTS

BODY HOOK

A body hook should be permanently attached to a pole at least 12 ft. in length. Some pools are missing body hook all together others do not have 12 ft in length as required.

LIFE RING

Provide a readily accessible life ring with an attached rope equal in length to the width of the pool shall be attached to the life ring. Some pools don't have life rings or the rope, at times they are not in good condition. You can contract with vendor that sells these rings at discounted price. Every swimming pool must have a life ring at least 17" in diameter and must be readily accessible. It must be 3/16 inch thick.

POOL SIGNAGE REQUIREMENTS

All signs are required; if they don't adhere to requirement you can suggest selling these signs to your clients. Many pools have frayed, and illegible signs that need replacing. As an optional service you can even offer to fill the signs for them at no charge.

All signs must be in a conspicuous place. All signs must have clearly legible letters or numbers not less than 4 inches high, unless otherwise noted, fixed to a wall gate or similar permanent structure in a location visible to all pool users and be clearly visible from the deck.

ARTIFICIAL RESPIRATION SIGN

Artificial respiration signs must now include CPR procedures. A diagrammatic illustration of artificial respiration procedures must also be posted.

EMERGENCY SIGN

Besides requiring "911" on an emergency sign, the sign must also include the number of the nearest emergency services and the name and street address of the pool facility. A telephone number of an emergency paramedic service shall be posted. This may be placed in the space provided on the artificial respiration sign if you are pressed for space.

NO LIFEGUARD ON DUTY SIGN

If there are no lifeguards on duty, a warning sign stating

"Warning – No Lifeguards On Duty" In addition, the sign shall state *"Childeren Under the age of 14 Should Not Use The Pool Without Adult In Attendance"*

NO DIVING SIGN:

At every swimming pool with a maximum depth of 6 ft. or less, a sign, stating

"No Diving Allowed"

SPA WARNING SIGN

"Spa Emergency Shut-Off Switch"

Every spa pool with an emergency shut-off switch shall have this sign legible.

You may also include

"Elderly persons, pregnant women, infants and those with health conditions requiring medical care should consult with a physician before entering a spa. Unsupervised use by children under the age of 14 is prohibited. Hot water immersion while under the influence of alcohol, narcotics, drugs or medicines may lead to serious consequences and is not recommended. Do not use alone. Long exposure may result in nausea, dizziness or fainting."

Emergency shut-off which requires an emergency shut-off switch, the switch shall be labeled with a sign stating "Spa Emergency Shut-off Switch.

Note the spa emergency shut-off switch shuts off all pumps, blowers and jet pumps in case of an emergency. Ensure that a sign is posted near the switch. Not all spas have an emergency switch; older spas were not required to have an emergency shut-off switch.

OCCUPANT CAPACITY SIGN

A sign stating the maximum occupant capacity must be posted in letters at least 4" high.

Maximum occupancy sign, you can even offer to calculate the occupancy.

Capacity can be calculated in following way:

Swimming pools = 1 per 20 sq.ft. of pool surface area.

Spa pool = 1 per 10 sq.ft.

Find the sq ft of the pool and do the above calculation. We will discuss calculations later in detail. You can offer to enter this in for your client. Sometimes the capacity is blank or not on letters that are at least 4" high.

KEEP CLOSED SIGN

This sign shall be posted on the exterior side of all gates and doors leading into the pool enclosure area stating,

"Keep Closed."

DIARRHEA NOTICE SIGN

A sign in letters at least 1 inch high shall be posted at the entrance area of a public pool which states that

"Persons having currently active diarrhea or who have had active diarrhea within the previous 14 days shall not be allowed to enter the pool water"

DAMAGED EQUIPMENT AND PARTS

During your regular pool maintenance you may notice broken or missing parts at the pool or pump room. All of these items should be in good working condition. If you have approved licensing you can opt to do this job yourself or make a referral to pool servicing company and be on their referral list.

List of commonly damaged items that are found at swimming pool:

- Unreadable depth marker tiles
- Damaged Coping
- Rough tiles inside pool
- Recirculation pump not working properly, gasping for air
- Influent / Effluent pressure gauge(s) are missing or not operating
- Flowmeter is stuck
- Skimmer weir assembly and skimmer strainer basket is broken
- Handrails, Grab rails and ladder steps are damaged

- Damaged drain cover which can only be removed with tools

- Automatic chlorinator is required-you can fix or sell one to your clients (floating chlorinator or chlorine tablet in pool are not allowed).

UNDERWATER LIGHT(S)

Underwater pool light(s) should be "on" during all times the pool is open for use after dark. If the pool is not separately enclosed, maintain pool light(s) on during entire nighttime hours. Underwater pool lights should be on during all nighttime hours unless the pool is completely enclosed with a fence around the immediate area of the pool. The light must always be on during nighttime hours when the pool is officially open for use. Pool hours must then be posted at pool side.

WATER HEATER

Showers and lavatories must have at least 110F of water minimum. However the <u>maximum</u> temperature allowed in a public spa is 104 F. There is no minimum temperature for SPA, but who wants a cold spa? Recommend fixing/installing properly rated water heater.

SHOWERS AND LAVATORIES

Fixed soap dispensers, soap dispensers are required in the bathroom.

POOL ENCLOSURES

Pool enclosure comprises of pool fence and/or a self-closing gate. If you see damaged enclosure or a door that remains open, I highly advice you recommend this service to your client not because it generates income every, however more as a safety precaution. Ever year many children are drowned. You could save a life!

For new pools, all parts of the fence enclosure fence around a pool shall be constructed over a hard and permanent material equivalent to concrete. The distance between the bottom of the fence and the hard permanent material shall not exceed 4 inches.

No planters or other structures that can be climbed shall be permitted within 5 feet of the outside of the pool enclosure or within a 5 foot arc. The area 5 feet outside of the pool enclosure shall be a common area open to the public.

LIVER TERMINALS:

A time clock mechanism's live terminals must be protected with the appropriate insulator/cover to prevent electrical shock.

TEST KIT

An approved pool water test kit is required at site you can offer to sell this to your clients.

RECIRCULATION PROBLEM

This book is not intended as a troubleshooting guide, however you may realize that pool at time is not recirculating water properly.

Remember the turnover rate is 6 hours for swimming Pools, 0.5 hours for spas and 1 hour for wading Pools. If your calculation doesn't add up to required turn over time, you can do some investigative work.

There could be many reason a pool/spa is not meeting this requirement. As a good technician you should be able to figure this out and provide a solution. It could be clogged filter, pump not working properly, etc... This is a service that can be added to recommended service.

Above are just some of the examples of services you can provide to your client. As a good service tech. you should takes 5-10mins to evaluate condition and provide needed service. Not only will they appreciate the extra effort you conducted but this can also build a better client/vendor relationship. This will eventually result in higher sales or just client appreciation of the extra effort you took in notifying them of the concerns.

Let them know you are conducting this inspection free of charge to help them comply with state regulations and this can also help them stay in compliance with state regulations.

CHAPTER 11:
POOL CALCULATION

Whether you have purchased this book to understand commercial pool regulations, improving sales of your business or in hopes of passing your local pool service technician license; you should know the basic pool formulas. These formulas are vital in understanding pool treatment options. Some require straight memorization and others require you to understand the concept and make meaning of the calculations.

GENERAL CONVERSION FORMULAS

*During exam most of this information would be provided to you.

1 gallon of water weighs 8.3 lbs.

1 gallon of liquid chlorine weighs 10.0 lbs.

1 pound per square inch equals 2.31 ft. of water (or feet of head).

1 inch of mercury equals 1.13 ft. of water (or feet of head). .

1 cubic foot equals 7.5 gallons.

1 horsepower equals 746 watts.

16 ounces = 1 pint (pt.)

16 ounces = 1 pound (lb.)

$A = \pi r2$

Circumference (C) = total perimeter of a circle

Total chlorine = combined chlorine + free chlorine

Power (watts) = volts x amps

Diameter (D) = line drawn from one edge to the other

Radius(R) = line drawn from the diameter midpoint to the edge of a circle forming a 90° angle

Required flow rate = pool volume (Turnover time x 60)

Required filter area = flow rate (GPM) per sq. ft.

Water loss = length x width x (loss in inches/12) x # of days x 7.5

Maximum bather load (pool) = Total surface area in sq. ft./20

Maximum bather load (spa) = Total surface Area in sq. ft./10

Chlorine residual= (pounds of product) x (% strength) x (1,000,000)

(In ppm) volume x 8.3

2 ounces of Muriatic Acid lowers the Total Alkalinity of 1,000 gallons of pool water 10 ppm.

0.083 lbs. of Cyanuric Acid raises the CYA level of 1,000 gallons of pool water 10 ppm.

0.15 lbs. of sodium bicarbonate raises the Total Alkalinity of 1,000 gallons of pool water 10 ppm.

BASIC POOL CALCULATION EXAMPLES

<u>Volume of rectangle pool = length x width x average depth x 7.5</u>

Therefore using the above formula it would be easy to calculate the number of gallons which are found in a rectangle pool. One would multiply the length by the width to obtain the surface area in square feet and then by the average depth to obtain the cubic feet and finally by 7.5 to obtain the number of gallons.

For example, a 20 x 40 pool with an average depth of 5 feet would have 20 x 40 x 5 x 7.5 = 30,000 gallon pool capacity. A more accurate calculation is possible if one divides the pool into three parts and calculates the gallon in the area from the shallow end to the break, the break to the main drain and the main drain to the deep end wall.

Example:

POOL IS 40 FT. LONG, 20 FT. WIDE, 4 FT. DEEP

VOLUME = 40 X 20 X 4 X 7.5

= 24,000 GALLONS

1 cu. ft. of water = 7.5 gallons

If depth varies, use average depth

Average Depth = depth 1 + depth 2 / divided by 2 depth numbers

Example:

Pool is 30 ft. long,

15 ft. wide, 3~ ft. deep at the shallow end and 5 ft. deep at the deep end.

Volume = length x width x average depth x 7.5

= 30 x 15 x 3~ + 5 x 7.5/divided by 2 (2 depth # - ~3 & 5 =4.25)

= 30 x 15 x 4.25 x 7.5

= 14,343.75 gallons

Volume of circular pool = radius x radius x 3.14 x average depth x 7.5

VOL = TT r 2 X DEPTH X 7.5, Water Displacement

Example:

SPA: 10FT. Diameter (Radius 5 FT.)

3 ft. Deep

200 Gallon Water Displacement

VOLUME = (3.14) X (5)2 X 3 X (7.5) - (200 gal)

= 1566.25 GALLONS

Calculation of Turnover Rate

Turnover Rate (Turnover - amount of time it takes for all the water in the pool or spa to go through the filtration system one time. Swimming pools - 6 hours (8 hours for pools built before 1982) Spas - 30 minutes. Wading pools - 1 hour)

Turnover Time in hours = (Pool Volume in gallons)

(Maximum pool user load per hour) x (75) Or 6 hours, whichever is less.

Required Turnover Time (minutes-if it's 6hrs that's 6 x 60=360mins)

Remember turnover Time = Volume Flow Rate

Example 1:

20,000 Gallon Swimming Pool

20,000 gallons/360 = 55.6 gpm or 56 gpm

Example 2:

1, 000 Gallon Spa

1 ,000 gallons /30 = 33.3 gpm or 34 gpm

1,000 Gallon Spa would have Flowrate = 33.3 G/PM

Example 3:

Using above calculation a 30,000 Gallon Swimming Pool, would have Flowrate = 83.3 GPM

30,000 gallons/360 min. = 83.3 GPM

<u>Surface Area</u>

Example 1:

Surface area of Rectangle or Square shape=Length x Width

Pool that is 40 FT. long, 20 FT. Wide

Surface area = 40 X 20 = 800 SQ. FT

Example 2:

Surface area of Circular shape pool = Pie r 2

Pie=3.14

r = radius of circle

Spa with 10ft. diameter

AREA = TT r 2

= (3.14) (5)2

= (3.14) (25)S

=78.5 sq. ft

<u>Occupant Capacity</u>

Example 1:

Occupant Capacity is 20 SQ FT for pool & 10 SQ FT for spa

Pool is 50 FT. X 20 SQ FT

First calculate the Surface area= 50 X 20 =1,000 SQ FT

1,000/20 =50 people maximum for pool

Example 2:

Spa is 10FT. diameter

Surface Area of circular shape= Pie r 2

3.14 X (5)2/10 = 78.5= 7.8

OR 8 people maximum

Calculate Saturation Index:

Saturation Index=pH + AF (Alkalinity Factor) + CF (Calcium Factor) + F (Temperature Factor)-12.1(Constant)

EXAMPLE:

pH =7.6

AF=150PPM

CF=300PPM

F=82

TDS CONSTANT=12.1

CHAPTER 12:

PRACTICE TEST

Before you take the exam, see if you can calculate the following calculations:

- The volume of swimming pools and spa pools

- Water loss in gallons given a drop in water level

- Required turnover for pools and spas

- Required filter flow rates for pools

- Required filter sizes

- Area of filter grids

- Total dynamic head of a recirculation system

- Horsepower of pool motors given voltage and amperage

- Chlorine residual, given a specific type of chlorine product, and the volume of a pool

- Required dosage of chlorine to reach breakpoint chlorination

- Dosage of a chlorine product necessary to "burn *off*" a specific chloramine level

- Dosage of neutralizer needed to eliminate excessive chlorine levels

- Dosage of soda ash needed to raise pH or acid to lower pH

- Dosage of Cyanuric Acid needed to raise to a specific level

- Saturation index

Let's take a practice exam:

1. What effect does Sodium Hypochlorite have on the pH of pool water?

   A Raises

   B. Lowers

   C. Does not have any effect

2. Chloramines can cause

   A. chlorine odor

   B. eye burning

   C. both A and B

3. A common name for Sodium Hypochlorite is

   A. muriatic acid

   B. conditioner

   C. liquid chlorine

4. Calcium hardness should be kept between

   A. 75 - 120 ppm

   B. 150 - 300 ppm

   C. 300 - 500 ppm

5. A Saturation Index of +0.9 indicates

   A. etching conditions

   B. balanced conditions

   C. scaling conditions

6. Which chemical measures free chlorine?

   A. Orthotolidine

   B. Phenol Red

   C. Oiethyl-P-Phenylene Oiamine

7. What is the weight of one gallon of water?

   A. 7.5 pounds

   B. 8.3 pounds

   C. 10 pounds

8. The filter that does the worst job at filtering small particles out of pool water is a

   A. high rate sand filter

   B. cartridge filter

   C. diatomaceous earth filter

9. Pools should be super chlorinated when chloramines exceed

   A. 0 ppm

   B. 2 ppm

C. 1.0 ppm

10. The Pool Code requires that the chlorine residual in public pools be maintained above

    A. 2 ppm

    B. 4 ppm

    C. 1 ppm

11. Return lines in a pool recirculation system are those which

    A. Return water to the pool

    B. Return water to the pump

    C. Supply water to the filter

12. The chemical name for Muriatic Acid is

    A. Hypochlorous Acid

    B. Hydrochloric Acid

    C. Sulfuric Acid

13. How many gallons are contained in a pool that is 40 feet long by 20 feet wide with an average depth of 4.5 feet?

    A. 18,000 gallons

    B. 27,000 gallons

    C. 32,000 gallons

14. A public swimming pool contains 30,000 gallons of water. What is the minimum size DE filter required by the State Pool Code?

    A. 42 sq.ft.

    B. 72 sq.ft.

    C. 166 sq.ft.

15. A DE filter contains three grid elements measuring 2 feet by 4 feet. What is the total surface area of the filter?

    A. 12 sq.ft.

    B. 24 sq.ft.

    C. 48 sq.ft.

16. The Pool Code requires that the chlorine residual in public pools be maintained above

    A..2 ppm

    B..4 ppm

    C.1 ppm

17. Pools should be super chlorinated when chloramine exceed

    A. 0 ppm

    B. 2 ppm

    C. 1.0 ppm

18 Return lines in a pool recirculation system are those which

A. return water to the pool

B. return water to the pump

C. supply water to the filter

19. The chemical name for muriatic Acid is

A.Hypochlorous Acid

B.Hydrochloric Acid

C.Sulfuric Acid

20. How many gallons are contained in a pool that is 40 feet long by 20 feet wide with an average depth of 4.5 feet?

A.18,000 gallons

B.27,000 gallons

C.32,000 gallons

21. A public swimming pool contains 30,000 gallons of water. What is the minimum size DE filter required by the State Pool Code?

A.42 sq.ft.

B.72 sq.ft.

C.166 sq.ft.

22 A DE filter contains three grid elements measuring 2 feet by 4 feet. What is the total surface area of the filter?

A. 12 sq.ft.

B. 24 sq.ft.

C. 48 sq.ft.

Extra Pt.:

Stabilizer Example:

A cartridge-filtered, 20,000 gallon pool with a starting cyanuric acid level of 35 ppm used 17 pounds of dichlor in 8 weeks. Water replacement during this period was 1,200 gallons (assume all was from evaporation). Estimate this pool's present stabilizer level.

Answer: 35 ppm initial plus 59 ppm added during the period = 94 ppm

If you feel you still need additional study material, look at the following resources:

ADDITIONAL STUDY MATERIAL

Additional Study Material

1. "Basic Training Manual, Part 1, Chemicals"

   Independent Pool and Spa Service Association, Inc. (ippsa)

   P.O. Box 15828

   Long Beach CA 90815-0828

   888-360-9505 ippsamail@aol.com www.ippsa.com

2. "Continuing Education Series, Pool Chlorination Facts"

   Independent Pool and Spa Service Association, Inc. (ippsa)

   P.O. Box 15828

   Long Beach CA 90815-0828

   888-360-9505 ippsamail@aol.com www.ippsa.com

3. "Everything You Always Wanted To Know About Pool Care"

   "Guide to Chlorine"

   "Guide to pH, Alkalinity, Water Testing and Water Balance"

   "Guide to Alternative Sanitizes"

   Service Industry News

   P.O. Box 5829

   San Clemente, CA 92674-5829

   (949) 366-9981

   www.poolspa.com/publications/sin/products.html

4. "Basic Pool and Spa Technology"

   Various other publications

   National Spa & Pool Institute

   2111 Eisenhower Ave.

   Alexandria, VA 22314

   (703) 838-0083

   www.nspi.org

5. "Pool/Spa Operator's Handbook"

   National Swimming Pool Foundation

   224 East Cheyenne Mtn. Blvd.

   Colorado Springs, CO 80906

   (719) 540-9119

   www.nspf.com

6. "Pool Operator's Manual"

   Washington State Public Health Association

   Other publications available

   National Environmental Health Association

   720 S. Colorado Blvd.

   Denver, CO 80246

   (303) 756-9090

   www.neha.org

CHAPTER 13:
SWIMMING POOL CODES AND REGULATIONS

It is important to understand that some of what you will be applying is backed by regulations. Depending on the country and the state you live in, your local jurisdiction maybe different. Most of the regulation I will be citing are referenced to commercial pools, not residential pools. I will be "pooling" my codes from State of California, you should check with your local jurisdiction. California tends to be stricter than most if not all other states; therefore I have used them as the standard.

I have cited and interpreted codes from:

1. Health and Safety Code for California (you can get your own copy at www.cdph.ca.gov); however most of the swimming pool regulations are sited in section 116025-116068.

2. California Code of Regulations-Title 22, Chapter 20.

To save you time and headache of reading all of them yourself, I have provided some that may be important to know of in your daily capacity of work and some that are needed to pass the exam here. However you do not need to memorize them. This will be more for your reference. This is not a complete list of regulations and is not all inclusive list but I feel it will help you understand commercial pool requirements better.

CALIFORNIA COODE OF REGULATIONS TITLE 24, CHAPTER 31B

3109B.2 Depth Marking Line

There shall be installed a straight line of slip-resistant tile, 4 inches (101.6 mm) wide of contrasting co or across the bottom of the pool where the water depth is 4 ~ feet.

Exception: Pools having a maximum depth of five feet or less shall riot be required to have a depth marking line.

3109B.3 Decorative Designs

Designs on the bottom or walls of the pool which are shaped in a form that might reasonably be mistaken for, or give the illusion of being a human form, shall be prohibited.

3109B.4 Water Depth Markers

3109B.4.1 General:

The water depth shall be clearly marked at the following locations:

(1) maximum depth,

(2) Minimum depth,

(3) Each end,

(4) At the break in the bottom slope between the shallow arid deep portions of the pool [see also Section 31 08B.4]

(5) On the perimeter of the pool at distances not to exceed 25 feet.

Exception: A spa or wading pool shall have a minimum of two depth markers indicating the maximum depth.

3109B.4.2 Location of Depth Markers

Depth markers shall be located on the vertical pool walls at each end and side of the pool at or above the water level. If a pool exceeds 20 feet in width, additional markers shall be located on the edge of the deck next to the pool.

Exception: If depth markers cannot be located on the vertical pool walls above the water line because of the pool design, the depth markers shall be located so as to be clearly visible to bathers in the pool.

3109B.1 Lane Markings

Slip-resistant lane lines or other markings at the bottom of the pool shall not exceed 12 inches in width.3109B.4.3 Tolerance. Depth markers shall be positioned to indicate the water depth accurate to the nearest 6 inches.

3109BA.4 Size of Markers

Depth markers shall:

1. Have numerals a minimum of 3 inches in height and of a color contrasting with the background,

2. Be made of a durable material that is resistant to weathering; and

3. Be slip-resistant when they are located on the pool deck.

3103B.1 Spa Pool

A spa pool is a pool, not used under medical supervision, that incorporates a water jet system, an aeration system, or a combination of the two systems, and which may also utilize artificially heated water. The surface water area of a spa pool shall not exceed 250 square feet and the water depth shall not exceed 4 feet (1219 mm).

3118B.2 Gates

Gates and doors opening into the pool enclosure shall also meet the following specifications:

1. Gates and doors shall be equipped with self-closing and self-latching devices. The self- latching device shall be designed to keep the gate or door securely closed. Gates and doors shall open outward away from the pool except where otherwise prohibited by law. Hand activated door or gate opening hardware shall be located at least 3 112 (1067 mm) feet above the deck or walkway.

2. Except as otherwise provided herein, gates and doors shall be capable of being locked during times when the pool is closed. Exit doors which comply with Chapter 10 shall be considered as meeting these requirements. EXCEPTION: Doors leading from areas of hotels and motels, as defined in Business and Professions Code Section 25503.16(b), which are open to the general public, e.g., restaurants, lobbies, bars, meeting rooms, and retail shops need not be self-latching.

3. The pool enclosure shall have at least one means of egress without a key for emergency purposes. Unless all gates or doors are so equipped, those gates and/or doors which will

allow egress without a key shall be clearly and conspicuously labeled in letters at least 4 inches (102 mm) "EMERGENCY EXIT".

4. The enclosure shall be designed and constructed so that all persons will be required to pass through common pool enclosure gates or doors in order to gain access to the pool area. All gates and doors exiting the pool area shall open into a public area or walkway accessible by all patrons of the pool.

3122B –Gas Chlorination Equipment Room

Compressed chlorine gas storage containers and associated chlorinating equipment, when installed indoors, shall be in a separate room of not less than one-hour fire-resistive construction and shall comply with all of the following sections.

3122B.1 Location. The room shall not be located in a basement or below ground.

3122B.2 Entry. The entry door to the room shall open to the exterior of the building or structure and shall not open directly towards the pool or pool deck.

3123B.1 System Description

Each pool shall be provided with a separate recirculation and treatment system designed for continuous recirculation, filtration and disinfection of the pool water. The system shall consist of pumps, filters, chemical feeders, skimmers or perimeter overflow systems, and all valves, pipes, connections, fittings and appurtenances.

3123B.2 Installation

All recirculation and treatment system components shall be installed according to this code and in accordance with the equipment manufacturer's written instructions.

3123B.3 Accessibility

All filters, valves, pumps, strainers and equipment requiring adjustment shall be readily accessible for repair and replacement.

3128B Filters

3128B.1 General Requirements

All filters, regardless of type, shall be designed and constructed to withstand normal and continuous use without deterioration which could affect filter operation. Each filter shall comply with all of the following provisions:

1. Maintain clean and clear pool water under anticipated operating conditions.

2. Structural or functional failures shall not permit the passage of unfiltered water.

3. Filtration surfaces shall be easily disassembled and inspected.

4. Filtration surfaces shall be easily restored to the design capacity.

5. Filter parts shall be capable of resisting electrolytic corrosion (galvanic electric currents) due to the use of dissimilar metals.

3128B.2 Maximum Pressure Drop

The maximum pressure drop of a pressure-type filter, measured from the filter housing inlet to the filter housing discharge, shall not exceed 3 pounds per square inch gage (psig) (20.68 kPa gage) when initially operating at design flow rate.

3128B.3 Installation

Each filter vessel and element shall be installed, piped and provided with necessary valves so that it can be isolated from the system for repairs and backwashed individually

3132B.1 General Design Requirements

Chemical feeder equipment shall comply with all of the following:

1. Equipment shall be capable of being easily disassembled for cleaning and repair.

2. Equipment shall be constructed of corrosion-resistant materials.

3. Equipment shall be constructed to permit repeated adjustments without loss of output rate accuracy if equipped with an adjustable output rate device.

4. Equipment shall be constructed to minimize a stoppage from chemicals intended to be used therein or from foreign materials that maybe contained in said chemicals.

3132B.2 Piping

Piping used for the chemical feeder and its auxiliary equipment shall be resistant to the chemical and erosion action of the chemicals intended to be used therein and shall be installed to permit cleaning or otherwise to prevent clogging of the parts with chemicals.

3132B.3 Installation.

The feeder and its auxiliary equipment shall be constructed and installed to prevent uncontrolled discharge or siphonage of chemicals and fumes directly into the pool, its recirculation system or the pool area.

3133B.1 Minimum Capacity

The disinfectant feeder shall be capable of supplying not less than the air into the recirculation suction piping system. This device shall not leak more than 3 gpm of water during normal operation.

3134B (formerly 2-9042) Pool Fittings

The pool shall be equipped with one or more skimming methods which when combined shall be capable of continually withdrawing not less than 75 percent of the required circulation capacity, to provide continuous skimming of the water surface, and to provide an overflow drainage system.

3134B.1 Surface Skimmers

Each surface skimmer shall comply with all of the following provisions.

1. The skimmer shall be of the built-in-type, recessed into the pool wall.

2. Each skimmer shall be individually adjustable for the rate of flow with either an external or internal device.

3. The skimmer weir shall automatically adjust to variations in the pool water level over a range of not less than 4 inches.

4. The skimmer shall be provided with an air-lock protective device which shall not permit leakage of air into the recirculation suction piping system. This device shall not leak more than 3gpm of water during normal operation.

5. Each skimmer shall be provided with a removable and cleanable screen or basket to trap large solids.

6. There shall be not less than one skimmer for each 500 square feet of pool water surface area, or fractional part thereof.

7. The skimmer shall be constructed with suitable materials and methods to withstand anticipated use conditions.

8. Each skimmer shall be located in relation to pool inlets to aid recirculation and skimming.

Exception: Skimmers shall not be used 2.S the required overflow devices on a pool with a water surface area.

3137B.1.1

Sand Filters. In accordance with applicable local regulations, the backwash water from a sand filter shall be disposed of to a storm drain or sewer system, dry well, or, when approved, such water may be disposed of by surface or subsurface irrigation.

3137B.1.2 Diatomaceous Earth Filters

The backwash waste water from a diatomaceous earth filter shall discharge into a receiving chamber installed to collect the waste diatomaceous earth mixture, or when approved such waste shall be permitted to be disposed of by other means such as to a sanitary sewer.

3137B.1.3 Piping

Sumps and drain piping shall have sufficient capacity to receive pool system backwash without overflow of the sump receiver.

3137B.1.4 Visual Indicator

A sight glass shall be installed on the waste water discharge line from a filter.

EXCEPTION: The sight glass shall not be required when an air-gap connection from the filter vessel to a sewer or other drainage system is clearly visible to the operator during actual backwash operation.

3137B.2 Prohibited Connection

No direct connection of the pool or its recirculation system shall be permitted with a sanitary sewer, storm drain or drainage system. When permitted by local regulations, discharge to a sanitary sewer shall be through an air-gap type separation.

3123B.1 System Description

Each pool shall be provided with a separate recirculation and treatment system designed for continuous recirculation, filtration and disinfection of the pool water. The system shall consist of pumps, filters, chemical feeders, skimmers or perimeter overflow systems, and all valves, pipes, connections, fittings and appurtenances.

EXCEPTION: Pools using fresh water equivalent in flow to the requirements of Section 3124B.

NOTES:

1. Fresh make-up pool water shall conform to the physical and bacteriological standards of California Code of Regulations, Title 22, Chapter 20, Section 65531.

2. Two spa pools shall be permitted to share one recirculation and treatment system providing the flow and chlorination feed rate to each spa pool is individually metered and adjustable.

3123B.2 Installation

All recirculation and treatment system components shall be installed according to this code and in accordance with the equipment manufacturer's written instructions.

3123B.3 Accessibility

All filters, valves, pumps, strainers and equipment requiring adjustment shall be readily accessible for repair and replacement.

3124B (formerly 2-9032) Turnover Time

The recirculation and purification system shall have sufficient capacity to provide a complete turnover of pool water in:

1. One-half hour or less for a spa pool.

2. One hour or less for a wading pool.

3. Two hours or less for a temporary training pool.

4. Six hours or less for all other types of public pools.

3125B (formerly 2-9033) Recirculation Piping System and Components

3125:B.1 Line Sizes

Piping systems, including all parts and fittings other than inlet devices shall be sized so that the flow velocity shall not exceed 10 feet per second, excepting that the flow velocity shall not exceed 8 feet per second in any copper piping or in any pump suction piping.

3125:B.2 Gauges for Filters

A gauge shall be provided on each filter influent and effluent line. Each gauge shall have a scale range approximately 1 times the maximum anticipated working pressure and shall be accurate within 2 percent of scale. A vacuum gauge shall be provided for suction-type filters.

3125:B.3 Flow Meter

The recirculation system shall be provided with a flow meter, accurate within 10 percent of actual flow.

3125:B4 Strainers

A hair-and-lint strainer shall be provided on the suction side of the recirculation pump. Exception: A pump used with a vacuum filter where the filter elements are not removed for cleaning.

3125:B.5 Backwash Piping

Piping, including necessary valves conforming to Section 3125B.l shall be provided for each filter vessel or element which is of a type requiring periodic backwashing.

3125:B.6 Valves

Valves shall be accessible for operation and repair and shall not be located under any required deck area surrounding a pool. Valves, or other approved means of control shall be installed on all recirculation, backwashing, and drain system lines which require shutoff isolation, adjustment, or control of the rate of flow.

Each valve shall be identified with appropriate markings affixed directly to or near the valve.

3126B (formerly 2-90.14) Recirculation Pump Capacity

3126B.1 Pumps shall have design capacity at the following heads:

1. Pressure Diatomaceous Earth---At least 60 feet.

2. Vacuum Diatomaceous Earth--- Twenty inches vacuum on the suction side and 40 feet total head.

3. Rapid Sand-At least 45 feet.

4. High Rate Sand-At least60 feet.

3118B.2 Gates

Gates and doors opening into the pool enclosure shall also meet the following specifications:

1. Gates and doors shall be equipped with self-closing and self-latching devices. The self- latching device shall be designed to keep the gate or door securely closed. Gates and doors shall open outward away from the pool except where otherwise prohibited by law. Hand activated door or gate opening hardware shall be located at least 3 112 (1067 mm) feet above the deck or walkway.

2. Except as otherwise provided herein, gates and doors shall be capable of being locked during times when the pool is closed. Exit doors which comply with Chapter 10 shall be considered as meeting these requirements.

EXCEPTION: Doors leading from areas of hotels and motels, as defined in Business and Professions Code Section 25503.16(b), which are open to the general public, e.g., restaurants, lobbies, bars, meeting rooms, and retail shops need not be self-latching.

1. The pool enclosure shall have at least one means of egress without a key for emergency purposes. Unless all gates or doors are so equipped, those gates and/or doors which will allow egress without a key shall be clearly and conspicuously labeled in letters at least 4 inches (102 mm) "EMERGENCY EXIT".

2. The enclosure shall be designed and constructed so that all persons will be required to pass through common pool enclosure gates or doors in order to gain access to the pool area. All gates and doors exiting the pool area shall open into a public area or walkway accessible by all patrons of the pool.

3118B.1 Enclosure

The pool shall be enclosed by one or a combination of one of the following: a fence, portion of a building, wall or other approved durable enclosure. Doors, openable windows, or gates of living quarters or associated private premises shall not be permitted as part of the pool enclosure. The enclosure, doors and gates shall meet all of the following specifications:

1. The enclosure shall have a minimum effective perpendicular height of 5 feet (1524 mm) as measured from the outside.

2. Openings, holes or gaps in the enclosure, doors and/or gates shall not allow the passage of a 4 inch (102 mm) diameter sphere. The bottom of the enclosure shall be within 2 inches (51 mm) of the finished grade.

3. The enclosure shall be designed and constructed so that it cannot be readily climbed by small children. Horizontal and diagonal member designs, which might serve as a ladder for small children, are prohibited. Horizontal members shall be spaced at least 48 inches (1219 mm) apart. Planters or other structures shall not be permitted to encroach upon the clear span area. Chain link may be used provided that the openings are not greater than 1 3/4 inches (44 mm) measured horizontally.

3114B Pool Lighting

3114B.l General

Where pool lighting is provided, it shall be such that lifeguards or other persons may observe, without interference from direct and reflected glare from the lighting sources, every part of the underwater area and swimming pool surface, all diving board or other pool appurtenances. NOTE: See (Part 3) Article 680 for electrical installation requirements.

3114B.2 Nighttime Use

Pools used at night shall be equipped with underwater light fixtures that will provide complete illumination to all underwater areas of the pool with no blind spots. Illumination shall enable a lifeguard or other persons to determine whether:

1. A bather is lying on the bottom of the pool, and

2. The water conforms to the definition of "clear pool water".

EXCEPTION: Pools provided with a system of overhead lighting fixtures, where it can be demonstrated to the enforcing agency that the system is equivalent to the underwater lighting fixture system.

3114B.3 Deck Area Lighting

Where the pool is to be used at night, pool deck areas shall be provided with lighting so that persons walking on the deck can identify hazards. Lighting fixtures shall be aimed towards the deck area and away from the pool surface insofar as practical.

3110B.2 Ladders

Ladders with a handhold shall be corrosion resistant and shall be equipped with slip-resistant tread surfaces. Ladders shall be rigidly installed and shall provide a clearance of not less than 3 inches (76 mm) or more than 5 inches (127 mm) between any part of the ladder and the pool wall.

3110B.3 Stairs

Each step of a stair shall have the same dimensions with a tread not less than 12 inches (305 mm) wide, except that if the top step is curved convexly, the top step tread shall not be less than 18 inches (457 mm) wide as measured at the point of maximum curvature. Risers shall be uniform and shall not exceed 12 inches (305 mm) in height. A safety railing shall be provided, extending from the deck to not less than a point above the top of the lowest step and the upper railing surface not less than 28 inches (711 mm) above the deck.

3110B.4 Steps and Step Holes

Steps and step holes shall have a minimum tread of 5 inches (127 mm), width of 14 inches (356 mm), and shall be designed to be readily cleaned.

3110B.5 Hand Railings

Hand railings shall be provided at the top of both sides and shall extend over twenty inches (508 mm) on side and 40 feet total. head.

3127B Water Supply Inlet

3127B.l General

The pool shall be supplied with water by means of a permanently installed pipeline from a public water supply system holding a permit from the Department of Health Services or from another approved source. EXCEPTION: The enforcing agency may exempt spa pools, temporary pools, and pools less than 1,500 gallons (5678L) capacity from having to use permanently installed fill lines.

3127B.2 Backflow Protection

There shall not be a direct connection between any domestic water supply system and the pool or its piping system unless protected against backflow in an approved manner.

3127B.3 Air-Gap Separation for Pool Fill Inlets

Water supply inlets to a pool shall be installed not less than 1 inch (25 mm) or less than two pipe diameters above the overflow rim of the pool. Over- the-rim spouts shall be installed under a diving board or shall be properly guarded to prevent tripping.

EXCEPTION: Vacuum breakers, or other backflow-prevention devices, may be used instead of air-gap separation. Such devices shall be installed on the discharge side of the last inlet valve with the critical level not less than 6 inches (152 mm) above the overflow rim of the swimming pool.

CALIFORNIA COODE OF REGULATIONS TITLE 22, CHAPTER 20

65501 Definitions

(a) "Swimming Pool" or "Pool" means an artificial basin; chamber or tank used, or intended to be used, for public swimming, diving, or recreative bathing, but does not include baths where the main purpose is the cleaning of the body, nor individual therapeutic tubs.

(b) "Wading Pool" means an artificial basin, chamber or tank used, or intended to be used, for wading by small children and having a maximum depth of not to exceed 46 centimeters (18 inches) at the deepest point nor more

(c) "Special Use Pools" means pools designed and used exclusively for a single purpose such as wading, instruction, diving, competition or medical treatment where a licensed professional in the healing arts is in attendance.

(f) "Spa Pool" means a pool, not used under medical supervision that contains water of elevated temperature, and incorporates a water jet system, an aeration system or a combination of the two systems. Spa benches must be a minimum of 12 inches but not more than 24 inches in width. The clearance between parallel benches in a spa must be at least 24 inches. The floors of spas are required to have a minimum length and width, or diameter of 24 inches.

65521 Pool Supervision Responsibility

(a) Every pool shall be under the supervision of a person who is fully capable of, and shall assume responsibility for, compliance with all requirements relating to pool operation, maintenance and safety of bathers.

(b) No pools shall be used or available for use unless all of the requirements of subsection (a) and the following are complied with.

(1) Routine (e.g., daily and weekly) operating procedures shall be permanently posted in a location accessible to and frequented by the operator.

(2) Manufacturers' instructions for operation and maintenance of mechanical and electrical equipment shall be kept available for the operator.

65523 Operation Records

(a) The operator of each pool open for use shall keep a daily record of information regarding operation, including readings of disinfectant residual, pH and maintenance procedures such as cleaning of filters and quantity of chemicals used.

(b) If cyanuric acid by itself or in a combined form with the disinfectant is added to a pool, the cyanuric acid concentration shall be measured a minimum of once per month and records shall be kept of the results of such testing

(c) Data collected pursuant to subsections (a) and (b) shall be maintained at least one year for inspection by the enforcing agent, or shall be submitted to the enforcing agent upon his request.

65533 Cleanliness of Pool

(a)   Floating scum, sputum or debris shall not be allowed to accumulate in the pool. Skimmers, where provided, and water levels shall be maintained and operated to remove such material continuously. The bottom and sides of the pool shall be cleaned as often as necessary to be kept in a clean condition. The sides and bottom of pools, decks and other surfaces shall be kept free of slime and algae.

(b) Animals shall not be permitted in the pool or pool area.

65535 Cleaning and Maintenance

(a) All parts of the pool and related pool facilities and equipment shall be maintained in good repair.

Floors shall be kept free from cracks and other defects and in compliance with Section 3115B, Title 24, and California Administrative Code. Walls, ceilings, partitions, doors, lockers and similar surfaces and equipment shall be refinished in a manner acceptable to the enforcing agent as often as necessary to be kept in a state of good repair.

(b) Hoses shall be provided for regular flushing and cleaning. The whole pool area shall be kept clean, sanitary and free of litter and vermin.

(c) Toilets, urinals, showers, wash basins and other plumbing fixtures shall be maintained in a clean condition, and in good repair.

68013. Emergency Switch for Spa Pools

A clearly labeled emergency shut-off switch for the control of the recirculation system and the aeration and/or jet system shall be installed adjacent to the spa pool.

65519. Disinfection

(a) Pools, when open or in use, shall be disinfected continuously by a chemical which imparts a residual effect and shall be maintained in an alkaline condition at a pH between 7.2 and 8.0. For pools using hypochlorite or gaseous chlorine without a stabilizer, a free chlorine residual at least 1.0 ppm shall be maintained throughout the pool. If cyanuric acid or a chlorinated isocyanurate is used, a free chlorine residual of at least 1.5 ppm shall be maintained throughout the pool. The cyanuric acid concentration in any pool shall not exceeded 100 ppm. Appropriate test kits for measuring the pH, concentration of the disinfectant, and, when used, concentration of cyanuric acid shall be provided at each pool. If halogens other than chlorine are used, residuals of equivalent strength shall be maintained. A test kit for measuring the concentration of the disinfectant accurate to within 0.1 ppm shall be available at each pool.

(b) When test kits for chlorine utilize comparative color standards, the standards should be accurate to within plus or minus 0.1 ppm. There shall be at least four color standards as follows: 0.6, 1.0, 1.5 and 2.0. The test kit shall be capable of testing for free chlorine residual,

(c) The enforcing agent may accept other disinfecting materials or methods after they have been demonstrated to provide a readily measurable residual. Such materials or methods must be as effective as the required chlorine concentration and must not be dangerous to public health or create objectionable physiological effects.

65525. Recirculation and Purification System Operation

The pumps; filters, disinfectant and chemical feeders, flow indicators, gauges and all related parts of the pool water purification system shall be kept in operation whenever the pool is available for use, and at such additional times and periods as may be necessary to maintain the water in the pool in a clear and disinfected condition.

65527. Clarity of Water

The recirculation and purification system shall be operated and maintained so as to keep the pool water clean and clear. Under no circumstances shall the pool be used if the main drain is not clearly visible from the deck. Such a pool shall be closed and shall not be reopened until the water is clean and clear, and upon specific written approval of the enforcing agent.

65533 Cleanliness of Pool

(a) Floating scum, sputum or debris shall not be allowed to accumulate in the pool. Skimmers, where provided, and water levels shall be maintained and operated to remove such material continuously. The bottom and sides of the pool shall be cleaned as often as necessary to be kept in a clean condition. The sides and bottom of pools, decks and other surfaces shall be kept free of slime and algae.

(b) Animals shall not be permitted in the pool or pool area.

65535 Cleaning and Maintenance

(a) All parts of the pool and related pool facilities and equipment shall be maintained in good repair. Floors shall be kept free from cracks and other defects and in compliance with Section 3115B, Title 24, California Administrative Code. Walls, ceilings, partitions, doors, lockers and similar surfaces and equipment shall be refinished in a manner acceptable to the enforcing agent as often as necessary to be kept in a state of good repair.

(b) Hoses shall be provided for regular flushing and cleaning. The whole pool area shall be kept clean, sanitary and free of litter and vermin.

(c) Toilets, urinals, showers, wash basins and other plumbing fixtures shall be maintained in a clean condition, and in good repair.

65539 Lifesaving, First Aid and Control of Bathers

(a) Lifeguard services shall be provided in accordance with Sections 116028 and 116045 of the Health and Safety Code.

(b) Where lifeguard service is provided, the number of lifeguards shall be adequate to maintain continuous surveillance over the bathers.

(c) Where no lifeguard service is provided, a warning sign shall be placed in plain view and shall state "Warning-No Lifeguard on Duty" with clearly legible letters at least 10.2 centimeters (4 inches) high. In addition, the sign shall also state "Children Under the Age of 14 Should Not Use Pool Without An Adult In Attendance".

(d) The enforcing agent may require posting of notices directing the bathers to make use of the toilets and showers before entering the pool. At all pools, diagrammatic illustrations of artificial respiration procedures shall be posted where clearly visible from the nearby deck. Such illustrations shall be protected against the elements. Also, the telephone number of the nearest ambulance, fire and police or sheriff department shall be kept similarly posted along with instructions that, if needed.

65541 Health of Employees and Patrons

(a) No person having a communicable disease shall be employed at a public swimming pool.

(b) All patrons known to be, or suspected by the enforcing agent or the management of being afflicted with an infectious disease, suffering from a cough, cold or sores, or wearing bands or bandages shall be excluded from all public bathing places unless at least one of the following conditions is met:

  (1) The patron submits a current written statement, signed by a licensed physician, confirming that the patron does not present a health hazard to other pool users.

  (2) Pool use by the patron is approved by the enforcing agent.

65549 Replacements of Equipment or Appurtenances

When fixed or installed equipment or appurtenances are changed or replaced, the change or replacement units shall meet applicable requirements of this Chapter subject to the provisions of Section 116050 of the Health and Safety Code, and shall first be cleared with the enforcing agent before substitution if not an exact duplicate of the units being changed or replaced.

65551. Shower, Toilet and Dressing Facilities

(a) For shower, toilet and dressing facilities, the walls, partitions, doors, lockers and similar surfaces which require periodic cleaning shall be maintained smooth and finished so as to facilitate cleaning.

(b) Showers shall be provided with soap in soap dispensers or containers.

680-12 Gas Chlorination Equipment Rooms

(a) Switch Location. Switches for the control of mechanical ventilation and lighting fixtures in a room used for gas chlorination equipment shall be located adjacent to the entry door outside of the room. Each switch shall be clearly labeled "Turn on before Entering".

(b) Equipment Interlocks. The gas chlorine feeding devices shall be interlocked with the pool recirculating pump so that the gas chlorine feeding devices shall not operate when the recirculating pump is off or during the filter backwash cycle.

680-13 Emergency Switch for Spa Pools

A clearly labeled emergency shut-off switch for the control of both the recirculation system and the aeration and/or jet system shall be installed adjacent to the spa pool.

CALIFORNIA HEALTH & SAFETY CODE

<u>116043 Sanitary, healthful and safe condition of pool, appurtenances</u>

Every public swimming pool, including swimming pool structure, appurtenances, operation, source of water supply, amount and quality of water recirculated and in the pool, method of water purification, lifesaving apparatus, measures to insure safety of bathers, and measures to insure personal cleanliness of bathers shall be such that the public swimming pool is at all times sanitary, healthful and safe. Also See 3115B, 3115B.4.1, *3115BA.2 and* 311SB.4.3.

<u>116045 Necessity of lifeguard service</u>

(a) Lifeguard service shall be provided for any public swimming pool which is of wholly artificial construction and for the use of which a direct fee is charged. For all other public swimming pools, lifeguard service shall be provided or signs shall be erected clearly indicating that such service is not provided.

(b) "Direct fee," as used in this section, means a separately stated fee or charge for the use of a public swimming pool to the exclusion of any other service, facility, or amenity.

<u>116045 Necessity of lifeguard service</u>

Lifeguard service shall be provided for any public swimming pool which is of wholly artificial construction and for the use of which a direct fee is charged. For all other public swimming pools, lifeguard service shall be provided or signs shall be erected clearly indicating that such service is not provided.

COMMON SWIMMING POOL DEFINITIONS

Backwash-The process of thoroughly cleansing the filter media and/or elements and the contents of the filter vessel.

Bather-A person using a pool and adjoining deck areas for the purpose of water sports such as diving, swimming, wading, or related activities.

Clear Pool Water- Pool water that is free from cloudiness and is transparent.

Clean Pool Water- Pool water that is free of dirt, oils, scum, algae, floating materials, or other visible organic and inorganic materials that would sully the water.

Corrosion Resistant-Capable of maintaining original surface characteristics under the prolonged influence of the use environment.

Deck- An area surrounding a pool which is specifically constructed or installed for use by bathers.

Drain-A fitting or fixture, usually at or near the bottom of a pool, through which water leaves the pool normally to the recirculation pump.

Effective Particle Size- The theoretical size of sieve (in mm) that will pass. 10 percent by weight of the sand.

Enforcing Agency- Means the Health Officer or Director of Environmental Health or their designated registered sanitarian representative.

Equipment Area- An area used for pool recirculation and purification equipment and related piping appurtenances.

Inlet-A fitting or fixture through which circulation water enters the pool.

Ladder-A series of vertically separate treads or rungs either connected by vertical rail members or independently fastened to an adjacent vertical pool wall.

Maximum Pool User Load- means the maximum number of persons allowed in a pool at any one time.

Medical Pool- A special-purpose pool used by a state-recognized medical institution engaged in the healing arts under the direct supervision of licensed medical personnel for treatment of the infirm.

Overflow System-The system which includes perimeter type overflow gutters, surface skimmers, surge or collector tanks, other surface water collective system components and their interconnecting piping.

Pools- A constructed or prefabricated artificial basin, chamber or tank intended to be used primarily by bathers, and not for cleaning of the body or for individual therapeutic use.

Pool User Load- means the estimated peak number of pool users per hour for a particular attraction at a Recreational Water Park.

Pool Volume-The amount of water, expressed in gallons (liters), that a pool holds when filled.

Private Pool-Any constructed pool, permanent or portable, which is intended for non-commercial use as a swimming pool by not more than three owner families and their guests.

Public Pool- A pool other than a private pool.

Recessed Steps -A riser/tread or series of risers/treads extending down into the deck with the bottom riser or tread terminating at the pool wall (thus creating a "stair well").

Recessed Treads-A series of vertically spaced cavities in the pool wall creating tread areas for step holes.

Recirculation System-The interconnected system traversed by the recirculated water from the pool until it is returned to the pool, i.e., from the pool through the collector or surge tank, recirculation pump, filters, chemical treatment, and heater (if provided), and returned to the pool.

Shallow Pool-A pool that has a maximum depth of less than six feet

Slip-Resistant-A rough finish that is not abrasive to the bare foot.

Step-A riser and tread

Stairs-A series of two or more steps

Treatment of Water-The process of conditioning and disinfection of pool water by means of a combination of filtration and the addition of chemicals to the water.

Turnover Time- The period of time in hours required to circulate a volume of water equal to the pool capacity.

Uniformity Coefficient-The ratio of theoretical size of sieve (in mm) that will pass 60 percent of the sand to the theoretical size of sieve (in mm) that will pass 10 percent.

Water Line-The water line shall be defined in one of the following ways:

(a) Skimmer system-The water line shall be the midpoint of the operating range of the skimmers.

(b) Overflow system-The water line shall be the top edge of the overflow rim.

REFERENCES:

Public health Los Angeles county, www.lapublichealth.gov

Florida Dept. Of Health

www.floridahealth.gov/

The 2016 Florida Statutes

CHAPTER 514

PUBLIC SWIMMING AND BATHING FACILITIES

ADHS & AACE:

AAC Title 9, Chapter 8, Article 8, "Public and Semi-Public Swimming Pools and Bathing Places",

ADEQ:

Title 18, Chapter 5, Article 2, "Public and Semi-Public Swimming Pools and Spas

Health Care Agency: Orange County, California; ochealthinfo.com/

State Dept. –Cal. Health and Safety Code:

Health and Safety Code for California; Most of the swimming pool regulations are sited in section 116025-116068.

Center of Disease Control: http://www.cdc.gov/

California State Department of Public Health (http://www.cdph.ca.gov/)

California Code of Regulations, Title 24 (Construction standards)

California Code of Regulations, Title 22 (Maintenance standards)

California Health and Safety Code -Swimming Pool Sanitation

California Building Code, Public Swimming Pool Design and Construction

Training of Lifeguards to Administer First Aid and CPR

California Code of Regulations: Title 22, Chapter 20 Public Swimming Pools

Title 24 of the California Code of Regulations, Part 2

California Code of Regulations Title 24, Article 680: 680-12.

California Conference of Directors of Environmental Health

Recreational Health Technician Advisory Committee- Ozone Generating Equipment Guideline

Made in the USA
Lexington, KY
29 August 2019